# Religion &
# Nationalism
# in Eastern Europe
# & the Soviet Union

Selected Papers from the Third World Congress
for Soviet and East European Studies
Washington, D.C.
30 October–4 November 1985

Sponsored by the
INTERNATIONAL COMMITTEE
FOR SOVIET AND EAST EUROPEAN STUDIES
and the
AMERICAN ASSOCIATION
FOR THE ADVANCEMENT OF SLAVIC STUDIES

General Editor   R. C. Elwood   *Carleton University*

### EDITORIAL COMMITTEE MEMBERS

# Religion & Nationalism in Eastern Europe & the Soviet Union

Edited by Dennis J. Dunn

Lynne Rienner Publishers    Boulder & London

Published in the United States of America in 1987 by
Lynne Rienner Publishers, Inc.
948 North Street, Boulder, Colorado 80302

and in the United Kingdom by
Lynne Rienner Publishers, Inc.
3 Henrietta Street, Covent Garden, London WC2E 8LU

**Library of Congress Cataloging-in-Publication Data**

Religion and nationalism in Eastern Europe and the
   Soviet Union.

   Bibliography: p.
   Includes index.
   Contents: Nationalism and religion in Eastern
Europe and beyond / D.J. Dunn—Polish-Jewish
relations, 1918–1939 / Edward D. Wynot, Jr.—The
Jews among the nations in Bohemia and Moravia—
[etc.]
   1. Nationalism—Religious aspects.  2. Nationalism—
Europe, Eastern.  3. Communism and religion—Europe,
Eastern.  4. Europe, Eastern—Religion.  I. Dunn,
Dennis J.
BL65.N3R44   1987      322.1'0947       87-10038
ISBN 1-55587-069-4 (lib. bdg.)

Printed and bound in the United States of America

The paper used in this publication meets the
requirements of the American National Standard
for Permanence of Paper for Printed Library
Materials Z39.48-1984. ⊗

# Contents

**Table**

# Foreword

The articles selected for publication in this volume were chosen from among those presented at the Third World Congress for Soviet and East European Studies held in Washington, D.C., from 30 October to 4 November 1985. The Congress, which was sponsored by the International Committee for Soviet and East European Studies and the American Association for the Advancement of Slavic Studies, attracted over 3,000 scholars from forty-one countries. This figure represents a twofold increase over the number of delegates who attended either the first congress in Banff, Canada, in 1974 or the second congress in Garmisch-Partenkirchen, West Germany, in 1980 and reflects the revival of Slavic studies throughout the world.

More than 600 papers were formally presented or distributed at the Washington congress. From among the substantial number submitted for possible publication in this series, the editorial committee has selected 160 to appear in fifteen volumes. Five volumes are being published in the social sciences; three by Cambridge University Press and two by Lynne Rienner Publishers. Five volumes devoted to history and literature are being published by Slavica Publishers, while the remaining five in education, law, library science, linguistics, and aspects of Eastern European history are appearing as part of established series or as special issues of scholarly journals. The titles of all these publications will be found at the end of this volume.

As general editor for the third congress I should like to express my sincere appreciation to Donald W. Treadgold, the program chairman, and Dorothy Atkinson, executive director of the AAASS, who were responsible for the efficient organization of the Washington congress; to Oskar Anweiler and Alexander Dallin, the past and current presidents of the International Committee, for encouraging the publication of these proceedings; and to Roger Kanet, the general editor for the first two congresses, whose advice has been invaluable to his successor. Thanks also are owed to the congress participants who submitted their papers for consideration, to the editorial committee that selected those to be published, and to the editors of the various volumes.

*R. C. Elwood*
General Editor

DENNIS J. DUNN

# Introduction

This book is an attempt to initiate the study of the relationship between religion and nationalism, subjects of study usually not connected, even though they are sometimes so intimately related in reality. As a pioneering effort, it offers new insights and valuable information. It also contains first-rate scholarship by some of the world's leading authorities on religion in Eastern Europe and the Soviet Union. On the other hand, it suffers from the usual characteristics of a joint effort and a ground-breaking probe: the essays are not balanced by chronology, geography, or subject.

The dilemma facing the editor and publisher is what to do in such a situation: to not publish and thus miss the opportunity to open the debate on the nexus between religion and nationalism, or to publish and weather the reviews that will say that the scholarship is excellent but that the essays are not related specifically enough to produce a coherent book. Happily, in this case, the editor and publisher found the challenge to start the debate on the relationship between religion and nationalism persuasive and compelling. What made it such, of course, were the quality of the individual studies and the realization that, even though an essay on Jewish assimilation in Moravia and Bohemia seemed quite different from an essay on the Ukrainian Catholic church in Poland after World War II, all the essays treated some aspects of the broad but unsurveyed tie between religion, nationality, nationalism, and ethnicity in the nineteenth and twentieth centuries.

The relationship between nationalism and religion is complex, varied, and desperately in need of study. Religion is with us to stay; and, for the foreseeable future, so is nationalism. These phenomena are, in many regions, inextricably linked and a thorough examination would produce insight into such questions as the resurgence of Islam, the phenomenal growth of religion in the Soviet Union, liberation theology in Latin America, and certainly the unrest and future direction of events in Eastern Europe.

This book is a modest beginning. It brings together the observations of some of the leading scholars of religion in Eastern Europe and the Soviet Union. It is a slim book, but, in this case, as E. F. Schumacher said, small is beautiful. The relationship of religion and nationalism is complex and can be approached from many different angles. The contributions here represent an attempt to open the question by focusing primarily upon Eastern Europe. The approach has been left up to the individual scholar, and thus there is great variety in methodology and perspective.

Chapter 1 opens the question and attempts to lay out the significance of the relationship between religion and nationalism, sets the stage for the specialized studies that follow, and, finally, suggests the direction of events in Eastern Europe and the Soviet Union by approaching these regions from the perspective of the nature of the relationship between religion and nationalism.

Edward Wynot then examines the attitudes of the Poles—state and people—toward Jews between 1918 and 1939. He examines the burgeoning anti-Semitism in Poland and its adverse effect on the economic well-being of the Jewish people in Poland. However, he also points out that Jewish culture flourished.

Fred Hahn continues the study of Jews in Eastern Europe. He focuses on the Jews' cultural contributions to Bohemia and Moravia. Then he shows how the Jews of these lands were torn between German and Czech nationalism.

John Basil examines a different side of the tie between nationalism and religion. He studies the way the tsarist government hoped to use nationalism in Germany for its own purposes. He shows the ambivalent attitude of the Russian Orthodox church and the Russian government toward the Old Catholic church in Bismarck's Germany, and reveals the struggle between religion, nationalism, and the demands of *realpolitik*.

Jure Krišto presents a sound, balanced analysis of the party's attitude toward the Roman Catholic church and of the church's position toward the Yugoslav Communist party. He stresses the role of Catholicism in Croatian nationalism, but also points out that Yugoslavia is multinational and that the church must be sensitive to this reality. At the same time, he emphasizes that the Communists wish to deny the historical role of the church among the Croatian people—an effort, he argues, that is destined for failure.

Finally, Bohdan Bociurkiw makes an extraordinary contribution. His essay contains a great deal of new information on the suppression of the Ukrainian Catholic church in Galicia after World War II, on the position of the Ukrainian Catholics in Poland, and on the fascinating, triangular nexus between Ukrainian nationalism, Polish nationalism, and the Catholic church. Some of the material in his paper is so informative and definitive that it will lead to the rewriting of works dealing with religion in the Ukraine.

# Religion &
# Nationalism
# in Eastern Europe
# & the Soviet Union

DENNIS J. DUNN

# Nationalism and Religion in Eastern Europe

Nationalism and religion in the minds of many Western scholars and statesmen appear to have very little in common. The reason, of course, is that religion is not considered to be a decisive political force in the world. It is recognized as important in some circumstances, but not critical, and, actually, is believed to be decreasing in significance as modernization—the fruit of science and reason—sweeps across the globe. Nationalism, on the other hand, viewed at least by some as one of the results of modernization, is a dynamic force that is transforming the world. If anything, in fact, it is thought that nationalism and religion are inherently in opposition and that one of the reasons for religion's decline is the success of secular nationalism.

This outlook is drawn largely from the Enlightenment writers, the materialist philosophers, and the positivist thinkers of the eighteenth and nineteenth centuries. The philosophers and makers of the French Revolution, the great catalyst of modern nationalism, did not think there was any connection between nationalism and religion, except an inverse one. Rousseau, Voltaire, Diderot, and Robespierre made it absolutely clear that "barbarism and religion," to use Gibbon's phrase, were being left behind and that the new age of liberty, equality, and fraternity—the age of nationalism and democracy—would be conspicuous by the absence of religion.

1

Undoubtedly, they would have found the subjects of nationalism and religion to be so mutually antithetical that they would have presumed it to be fatuous even to try to relate them. They could not have conceived of a meaningful, let alone essential, role for religion in the national state. They blamed religion for many of the world's problems and looked forward to the day when religion would be finally exorcised from society. Gibbon even went so far as to hold Christianity responsible for the fall of Roman civilization. It was Gibbon who, in his brilliant book *The History of the Decline and Fall of the Roman Empire,* led the attack against religion, particularly Christianity. He was masterfully backed up by the writers of the French Enlightenment and the English Manchester School who thought they had forever banished God—"the Great Clockmaker" or "the Great Spectator"—from human affairs. Later in the nineteenth century, the Positivists and the materialist philosophers continued the attack and felt that they had debunked religion and proven that economics or politics were the *sine qua non* of the civil order.

The legacy of the eighteenth and nineteenth centuries regarding religion has carried over into the twentieth century. There continues to be a rather general view that religion is not really vital and, of course, when applied to the problem of nationalism, has a small part. Now this view is held despite numbing evidence that there is an innate religious impulse in man and that when this impulse is suppressed it finds an outlet, sometimes in the form of violent secular religions and dehumanizing wars. Furthermore, virtually no nationalist movements have succeeded without addressing religion, and, finally, religion is often a wellspring of national sentiment.

Did not the French revolutionaries, who attacked religion, ultimately transform nationalism and democracy into bloodstained, secular religions? Did not Marxism become a cruel creed, more orthodox and dogmatic than many religions? Did not World War I, World War II, and the advent of communism, nazism, and fascism offer some evidence that a godless world or, worse yet, a world where man played God was a barbaric world where the only order was disorder? Was not religion a basic factor in creating new national states or causing nationalist tensions among religiously different peoples in multinational states? It was for religious reasons that Pakistan and India split, and it is for religious reasons that civil war reigns in Northern Ireland and in Lebanon. It is for religious causes that Israel and her fellow Semitic but Muslim neighbors wage war; religion is a factor in the war between Iraq and Iran and between Afghanistan and the Soviet Union.

Are not Khomeini, Nasser, and Khadafy really desert raiders in the best tradition of the *jihad*? Is not the pope a Polish nationalist? If religion is so insignificant, how does one explain the burgeoning religious movements in Romania and the Soviet Union or the strength of the underground Ukrainian Catholic church and the Lithuanian Catholic church? How is the rising tide of Islamic fundamentalism or the growing Christianization of Africa explained? Why is it that both the government and left-wing guerrillas in El Salvador look to the bishop for support? Why does Moscow want the Vatican to support its foreign policy initiatives, from the Nuclear Non-Proliferation Treaty to the Helsinki Agreement?

Curiously, modern savants adopt the views of the eighteenth and nineteenth centuries over the insights of some of the greatest thinkers in history. Plato and Aristotle, for example, watched Greek civilization unravel and decline. They recognized that traditional morality had given way to the narrow interests of the *polis* and that there was no common system of beliefs that encouraged the Greeks to sacrifice private gain for the common good. Plato offered his mystical insights and Aristotle his aspiration after the Supreme Good, but their plans for a righteous order were rejected. The Greeks failed to develop a popular religion providing order and legitimacy for their civilization and a framework for overcoming the narrow interests of the *polis* in favor of the commonweal. Greek hubris knew no restraint, not even the threat of self-destruction. Plato's *Republic* is essentially a moral book that argues persuasively that order in society must come from order in the soul. Polybius, too, stressed the importance of religion. He was not a moral philosopher; in fact, he was, like many Greeks, quite skeptical about religion, but that made his analysis all the more important. Polybius informs us about both the rise and the fall of Rome: he correctly attributed Rome's vigor to its traditional religion and its emphasis upon virtue and piety, but at the same time he chronicled the inadequacy of that religion to serve as a basis for the empire.

Cicero and Vergil confirmed Polybius' description. They appealed forlornly to the Romans to restore the traditional religion or, in the case of Cicero, to adopt the moral philosophy of Stoicism in order to restore order; but the traditional religion was both inadequate and, alas, neglected, and Stoicism was too intellectual for the masses. Christianity, for its part, was too embryonic to save the empire—it did not, despite Gibbon's brilliant argument to the contrary, cause Rome's downfall—but it did provide a foundation for the new order of European civilization that followed Rome.

Of course, not all scholars in the twentieth century think religion is dying or insignificant vis-à-vis nationalism. Historians like Christopher Dawson, Eric Voegelin, Arnold Toynbee, and Russell Kirk have argued anew that religion, myths, or beliefs are the basis of all order, both private and public, but, needless to say, theirs are voices in the wilderness. The prevalent view continues to be that religion is far behind economics or politics in determining principles of order.

My purpose is to show that there is a connection between nationalism and religion, that religion is absolutely fundamental to order, that nationalism and religion in Eastern Europe are closely linked, at least for the time being, and, finally, that nationalism and religion have an impact on one another around the globe. Needless to say, the task is formidable, and I can at best only hint at the tremendous complexities of these subjects, especially the last one.

All of my efforts, of course, deal with nationalism and religion. So it is those two subjects that afford me a framework for dealing with the task at hand. Here definitions are in order. I turn first to nationalism and basically follow the definition that Norman Davies has sketched in his superb study of Poland.[1]

In the two centuries after the French Revolution, nationalism has been certainly one of the most powerful political and social forces in the world. It is a complex movement that requires careful distinctions if we are to talk about it intelligently. It is tied to the concepts of nationality, national consciousness, nation, and nationalist. Each of these terms must be defined in order to come to grips with nationalism. Nationality is basically a conviction, a profound belief about one's personal identity, that one belongs to a particular national group. It is not innate to humankind, and in European history is difficult to find in any time before the French Revolution. It has become in the past two centuries the central political and social force in many parts of the world, and is especially significant in Eastern Europe. It might be based on incorrect premises about common roots, as some have argued, like Ernest Renan, who says "a nation is a community united by common error with regard to its origins, and by common aversion with regard to its neighbors," but that seems to make little difference. It has taken on a life of its own. The nation, in turn, is the social group whose members, being persuaded correctly or incorrectly of their common ancestry and destiny, hold to that common idea of identity. National consciousness is the gauge of the people's awareness of their membership in the nation. Nationalism, consequently, is a doctrine held by all political groups that aim to set up and maintain a nation by stirring people's consciousness of their nationality, and to shape their aspirations into a movement for political action. In this context, a nationalist is a person who agrees with or argues for the goals of nationalism. In effect, nationalism is a means to organize or reorganize a state—a basis providing legitimacy to the process of fashioning or refashioning a state. Nationalism in and of itself is neither good nor bad. At times it can be democratic or undemocratic, fanatical or moderate, productive or destructive. The only thing that nationalists hold in common is the belief that nations have a right to determine their own destinies. For historians, nationalism is a phenomenon that can only be described; others must determine its morality.

Religion is quite different from nationalism. Many argue that religion is inherent in humans, that it is a response to people's need to feel secure about the future, the unknown, and the unknowable. In fact, as mentioned earlier, some of the most influential thinkers in history, such as Moses, Plato, Cicero, Vergil, Augustine, Aquinas, Pascal, and T. S. Eliot, hold that religion or beliefs are the basis of all order, including, of course, any order infused with nationalism. However, in studying the insights of these philosophers it becomes apparent that an important distinction must be made between religion or beliefs dying of themselves, i.e., proving to be inadequate to maintain order, and communities rejecting or abandoning religion and cutting society loose from its moral anchors, thereby bringing on disorder. The former is a failure of the religion while the latter is a failure of humans; both cases have precedents in history.

There are many religions throughout the world, and they are as complex and diverse as the people who profess them. For the sake of simplicity, I use the term to refer only to what theologians and philosophers call the "higher religions." Those are the ones that embody a principle of transcendence, i.e., a concept, sometimes a godhead, that involves human beings in an experience beyond the satisfaction of their immediate personal and social needs, an experience known as "the sacred" or "the holy"; these include Orthodox Christianity, Catholicism, Protestantism, Judaism, Islam, Buddhism, and Hinduism. Some would also include in this group Taoism and Brahmanism, and I certainly will not gainsay them.

While some might not accept the innateness of religion to humanity, no one seems to dispute the fact that religion has always been a part of human history and shows every sign of persisting into the future, although many Western scholars, as stated, assume that its role will be increasingly minimal. Even one Marxist author, James Thrower in his book *Marxist-Leninist Scientific Atheism*, now admits that some seem to need religion and, as a consequence, concludes that it will not likely ever wither away.[2] It seems to be a staple of the human condition, like politics or economics.

Generally speaking, the higher religions do not prescribe a certain political order. They are primarily concerned with human spiritual life, and they have coexisted with autocracies, monarchies, oligarchies, aristocracies, dictatorships, democracies, republics, and some totalitarian regimes. Yet they and other religious beliefs are absolutely crucial for the stability and viability of the political order. "We are only just beginning," Christopher Dawson remarks, "to understand how intimately and profoundly the vitality of a society is bound up with its religion."[3] But every case is different, and churches in one country will have a completely different outlook on political issues than their coreligionists in another country. The Catholic church in the United States, for example, espouses a different attitude about nationalism than the Catholic church in Poland. When it comes to the world of Islam, even though it is impossible to separate politics and religion and even though nationalism is repudiated in favor of a universal Muslim brotherhood, there are secular and religious governments, splits between Shiite and Sunni Muslims, and definable and separate national interests. This is a very complicated story, and it needs examination. Our primary concern now is with the broad relationship between religion and nationalism.

Religion, of course, existed quite nicely for thousands of years before nationalism appeared on the stage of human history, so we can safely say that religion is not a consequence of nationalism. In the East and West "man's primary and fundamental allegiance," writes Christopher Dawson, "was not to his nation, but to his religion." Humans thought of themselves, in other words, as Catholics, Jews, Muslims, Protestants, Hindus, Buddhists, Orthodox, or Sikhs, rather than as Italians, Frenchmen, Egyptians, Germans, Syrians, Russians, Indians, or Indonesians.[4]

Well then, is nationalism a consequence of religion? That is an interesting question, but it is really not the essential question, because in answering it we would find that, yes, in some parts of the world nationalism is strongly influenced by religion, but, alas, in other parts of the world it is not. We can say that nationalism is a relatively new movement that may or may not last, but, as long as it is an expansive movement that seeks to reorganize human relationships, it has had to and will have to come to terms with religion. It simply cannot relate to human beings without dealing with religion any more than it could if it failed to address politics or economics. There is, in other words, a direct and continuing tie between nationalism and religion.

The key question then is what is the relationship between nationalism and religion? First off, it is obvious that it varies in different parts of the world; furthermore, it has changed in certain areas in recent times. To give a complete survey of the history of the relationship of nationalism and religion around the world from, say, the time of the French Revolution to the present would fill a large book. My intention here is to discuss generally the relationship as it is in some parts of the world in order to suggest its complexity and the value of pursuing the study in a broader and more sophisticated fashion and, then, to focus on the relationship in Eastern Europe. I am afraid, as indicated earlier, that religion is usually bypassed as a subject of serious study because many scholars think of it as unimportant. I hope to suggest that that view is wrong and prevents understanding of human societies, especially in Eastern Europe and the Soviet Union.

First, let us examine the Anglo-Saxon democracies. Interestingly, in contrast to other parts of the world (especially Eastern Europe, Ireland, and, perhaps, Spain), religion is strong and nationalism is latent, if not weak. Because of the materialism of the Anglo-Saxon democracies, it is often overlooked that their leaders officially act in accordance with the moral habits of thought that are rooted in the Judeo-Christian heritage.[5] Individual leaders might be worldly and amoral, even immoral, but their official behavior is guided by laws and institutions that are firmly based on Judeo-Christian morality and constantly reaffirm a belief in a higher order. The North Americans, in particular, are very religious: Alexis de Tocqueville was struck by the close tie between religion and democracy in the United States. He could not get over the fact that these two powerful forces, which were virtually at odds everywhere on the continent of Europe, meshed and mutually supported one another in the United States. Paul Johnson, the former editor for *Realities* and *The New Statesman*, marvels, too, in a recent issue of *The Wilson Quarterly*, at how "religion and politics are organically linked in America" and that this marriage is a source of the United States' strength.[6] And, as all students of U.S. history know, U.S. foreign policy often takes on the dimension of a religious crusade, sometimes in combination with a pitiful ignorance of other people's religious culture, as when President William McKinley decided to Christianize the Philippines, the only Christian nation in Asia. In fact, the very strength of religion within the legal, political, and social fabric of the Anglo-Saxon democracies seems to explain, in part, why nationalism generally recedes into the background. This is not to say that nationalism is weak in the Anglo-Saxon democracies, especially in the United States—in fact, it seems to be surging into prominence under Ronald Reagan and Margaret Thatcher—but it is to say that nationalism is not an overwhelming passion in the Anglo-Saxon countries, except in times of national crisis. Generally, the Anglo-Saxon countries rely upon their institutions and laws rather than a national ideology to hold their state together, and religion is at the heart of these laws and institutions. Religion in the Anglo-Saxon democracies supports the view of nationalism as an undemocratic and illiberal movement that promotes disruption and revolution. This viewpoint holds that nationalism is not now and never will be a stable embodiment of law, morality, and tradition on which order and security are built. That nations cannot be states is a common assumption fostered by religions in Anglo-Saxon states, and it is a view that is quite characteristic of Western statesmen. Lord Acton phrased it well when he said "a state can sometimes create a nation, but for a nation to create a state is going against nature."

Unfortunately this antipathy toward nationalism has made Anglo-Saxon leaders, especially the Americans, reluctant to support nationalism or national movements in other parts of the world, particularly in Eastern Europe. They hold that nationalism in Eastern Europe, for example, is a terribly disruptive, even violent, development that could, if supported, lead to war. It is far better, in their view, to try to reform the established state, whether it be a dynastic or totalitarian empire or a military dictatorship, than to encourage national liberation movements.

The experience of Eastern Europe, however, flies in the face of the Western view: for the past two centuries, nationalism has been the driving force of change in Eastern Europe, and the attitude toward it has been quite different. It is viewed as a movement that will bring about in Eastern Europe the principles by which Western statesmen live. "It is depressing to realize," as Norman Davies has written, "that western liberals have an unfortunate tendency to take the side of the powers-that-be against the very people in Eastern Europe who most nearly share their own principles."[7]

Curiously, even though religion is at the root of the Anglo-Saxon democracies and U.S. foreign policy seems at times to be a religious crusade, statesmen in these countries act as if religion were an unimportant force elsewhere in the world. This is a true dichotomy. Religion is affirmed in their institutions, but they refuse to see its value and strength elsewhere. In a recent article in *The Intercollegiate Review*, Thomas Molnar attributes this outlook to the fact that Western governments are administered by businessmen and lawyers with a positivistic outlook.[8] This attitude has unfortunate repercussions. It can lead, for example, to advising the shah of Iran to proceed with modernization policies and not worry about the mullahs, and to believing that the Islamic republic is an aberration that will disappear when the Ayatollah Khomeini dies.[9] It can lead to missing the connection between religion and the political order in the Muslim communities of Morocco, Tunisia, Soviet Samarkand, Yugoslavia, Pakistan, and Bulgaria, and the Catholic communities in the Philippines, El Salvador, and Nicaragua. Those in the United States still don't seem to realize that the powerbroker in El Salvador is Archbishop Rivera y Damas and that the Catholic church is the key institution in Nicaragua.[10] In contrast, it is interesting to note that the Soviets are paying some attention to this connection: when the wife of the recently deposed President Marcos of the Philippines visited Moscow in 1985, they treated her like royalty and arranged for her to sing the "Ave Maria" in a church in Moscow.[11]

Moving from the Anglo-Saxon democracies to some of the

other countries of Western Europe, we find another variation in the relationship between nationalism and religion. In France and Italy, both nationalism and religion were strong, but nationalism was essentially antireligious because the dominant religion, in both cases the Catholic church, supported a status quo that the nationalists wished to change. The nationalists were able to marshal popular support against the church and to separate the church from the state. Today, the governments and the church coexist, but the societies are quite secular and the hold of the church seems to be weakening among the people as a whole. Since the institutions, as in the Anglo-Saxon democracies, are based upon Judeo-Christian principles, the decline of the church's influence might not augur well for the stability of the established order. If roots are not watered, they soon decay and die, and, in the words of Hannah Arendt, "the rootless are always violent." The Czech novelist Milan Kundera, now living in Paris, finds the West to be a cultural vacuum, and, not unlike Alexander Solzhenitsyn, believes the essential problem is that mankind has decided to play God.[12] In many ways, he is warning the nationalists that an antireligious orientation is self-destructive.

In Eastern Europe, we discover yet another alteration in the tie between nationalism and religion. For most of their modern history, the countries that now make up Eastern Europe were little more than names. They were part of empires where the Austrians, Russians, Turks, or Prussians were the dominant groups. However, they virtually all were viable as political ideas. The idea of Poland, Hungary, the Ukraine, Romania, Bohemia-Moravia, Croatia, Bulgaria, and Serbia had significance in history. The historian of Eastern Europe must concentrate on people's beliefs and hopes, on the development of the concept of Eastern European nations in lieu of Eastern European states.

In contrast to the citizens of Western democracies, where nationalism, if used at all, usually means support for the state and its policies, the East Europeans obtained their modern notion of nationalism in defiance of the state and its policies. Through much of modern history, the ruling states in Eastern Europe have attempted to suppress the various manifestations of Eastern European nationalism. The Eastern European nations were mainly gathered from people who, while admitting that they were Turkish, Prussian, Austrian, or Russian subjects, persistently denied that they were Turks, Prussians, Austrians, or Russians. In such conditions, Eastern European nationalism was pushed by nationalists who were actively opposed to the state. The distinction between citizenship and nationality is a major feature of East European life, which unfortunately is often blurred by Westerners who, for example, refer to all the peoples of the Soviet Union as "Soviets" or "Russians."[13]

The basic fact is that the modern nations of Eastern Europe are the consequence of modern Eastern European nationalism. Their growth has evolved sporadically for the past two hundred years, and their final success was far from secure for most of that time. Each Eastern European nation is different and complex, of course, and the time when nationalism played a decisive role in each varies and is debatable.

Because the Eastern Europeans lacked for most of modern history a national state, national consciousness drew on a variety of sources of inspiration, including religion, language, history, and race. It appears, in fact, that religion was the key factor influencing the formation of nations in the Balkans and Eastern Europe. Although political states eventually emerged as the framework of nations in that part of the world, the basis of order in the political state was and is religion. Besides, nationalism in Eastern Europe was and is essentially proreligious. This is a fundamental fact that is not often appreciated or understood by secular or unsympathetic observers. It is that way because in some Eastern European countries there were, as already mentioned, no national states. Instead, what we might call the national regions were part of larger empires, and, in this context, religion helped define people's nationality. This is certainly true in Poland and Lithuania, and I think a case can be made for Romania, Bulgaria, Serbia, Slovakia, Croatia, and Albania. Religion helped explain who belonged and who did not by distinguishing among true believers, heretics, schismatics, and infidels.

Another reason for the strong tie between nationalism and religion is that religion today opposes, in some countries, the communist order that Eastern European nationalists wish to change. This is particularly true of the Catholic church in Poland. One can argue similarly about the Catholic church in Lithuania and the suppressed Catholic church in the Ukraine. In a more general sense, all the religions in the various Eastern European communist countries are, ipso facto, challenges to governments that advocate atheism as part of their official ideology. If we were to borrow the insights of such moral philosophers as Plato, Aristotle, Confucius, Cicero, Vergil, Dostoevskii, and Tolstoi, we would have to say that order in the state and legitimacy for governments ruling the state ultimately come from religion or moral beliefs, that nationalism is a political movement that provides a new way of organizing or reorganizing the state but cannot provide enduring legitimacy or the motivation for people to support the state, and, finally, that there will be decay, unrest, and instability if there is not a belief system providing moral fiber. The Czech lands are a case in point. Of all the Eastern European states, secularism has advanced most dramatically in Czechoslovakia, but what does that say about the long-term future of the Czech lands? Does the lack of religious strength explain why the Czechs were in a position where they could only submit in 1938, 1948, and 1968?

An additional explanation for the proreligious nature of Eastern European nationalism is that some of the religions, notably Protestantism and Catholicism, give nationalists a tie to European culture. In his recent article in *Encounter* entitled "What Is Europe, Where Is Europe?" the late Hugh Seton-Watson asserted that "the truth is that nowhere in the world is there so widespread a belief in the reality, and the importance of an European cultural community, as in the countries lying between EEC territory and the Soviet Union." And he went on to say that "none of them can survive without Europe, or Europe without them," and that the key to European culture is Christianity.[14]

Finally, we must note that nationalism and religion have a bond in Eastern Europe because some nationalists are genuinely religious, and look to the church to care for their spiritual needs. This is a point of view that must be appreciated, especially by those scholars who are not religious themselves.

In summary, the relationship between nationalism and religion is complex, varied, and absolutely in need of study. Religion is with us to stay and, for the foreseeable future, so is nationalism. These phenomena are inextricably linked in many regions, and a thorough examination, I am sure, would reveal many insights into such questions as the resurgence of Islam, the phenomenal growth of religion in the Soviet Union, liberation theology in Latin America, and certainly the unrest and future direction of events in Eastern Europe. One might hazard to say that regimes that have abandoned or neglected their religious roots are inherently unstable, and that their future might not be unlike that of the shah of Iran. The Soviet Union and

Yugoslavia, of all the communist regimes in Eastern Europe, have managed to forge a tie between nationalism and the government, but that was due to special circumstances. It was the Nazi threat in the case of the Soviet Union, and World War II and, later, the Soviet threat in the case of Yugoslavia, but these circumstances are passing despite the best efforts of, for instance, the Soviet regime to have every schoolchild relive the war. As these circumstances become distant memories, and if religious persecution continues, decay and political instability might very well lie in the future. The expectation then is that we will see developing unrest in the Soviet Union and the Eastern European communist countries or, alternatively, the governments will increasingly accommodate themselves to the dominant religion. If it is the latter, then voices like Solzhenitsyn will be not the exception, but increasingly the rule; however, even he cannot save the non-Orthodox parts of the Soviet empire. Similarly in Eastern Europe: Poland's Solidarity will be seen not as an aberration, but the wave of the future in many parts of Eastern Europe; or, if the religious roots are abandoned or neglected, the Czechoslovak experience might await the Eastern Europeans.

At any rate, the tie between religion and nationalism is a subject that we neglect at our peril. There is much work yet to be done.

## Notes

1. Norman Davies, *God's Playground: A History of Poland*, 2 vols. (New York: Columbia University Press, 1982), 2: 5, 9–10.

2. James Thrower, *Marxist-Leninist Scientific Atheism* (Berlin–New York–Amsterdam: Mouton, 1983), 389.

3. Christopher Dawson, *Progress and Religion: An Historical Enquiry* (London: Sheed and Ward, 1929; reprint ed., Westport, Conn.: Greenwood Press, 1970), 232.

4. Christopher Dawson, *Christianity in East and West*, John J. Mulloy, ed. (La Salle, Ill.: Sherwood Sugden and Company, 1981), 187.

5. A. James Reichley, *Religion in American Public Life* (Washington, D.C.: Brookings Institution, 1985).

6. Paul Johnson, "The Almost-Chosen People," *Wilson Quarterly* 9(Winter 1985): 89.

7. Davies, *God's Playground*, 2: 5.

8. Thomas Molnar, "Islam on the Move," *The Intercollegiate Review* 21 (Fall 1985): 21–22.

9. For good, recent studies, see Dilip Hiro, *Iran Under the Ayatollahs* (Boston: Routledge and Kegan Paul, 1985), and Robin Wright, *Sacred Rage: The Wrath of Militant Islam* (New York: Linden Press, 1985).

10. Both the government and the guerrillas in El Salvador trust Archbishop Rivera. See, for example, *Christian Science Monitor*, October 25, 1985, 12. And it is for no strange reason that the Sandinistas have included two priests in their government and that the pope's visit to Nicaragua shook the government to its foundation.

11. All of this was done, of course, against the background of Washington's criticism of Marcos. For commentary, see *Wall Street Journal*, November 25, 1985, 1.

12. *Christian Science Monitor*, September 6, 1985, B5.

13. Davies, *God's Playground*, 2: 11.

14. Hugh Seton-Watson, "Where Is Europe, What Is Europe?" *Encounter* 65 (July/August 1985): 9–17.

# 2

EDWARD D. WYNOT, JR.

# Polish-Jewish Relations, 1918–1939: An Overview

The scholar attempting to unravel the complexities of the Polish-Jewish relationship in the interwar years, and then transmit his findings within a brief chapter such as this, inevitably confronts the necessity of being concise without losing or diluting the essence of his main points. The challenge is heightened by the growing body of well-researched, sound scholarship on this theme that has appeared in the past two decades. Therefore, in order to do the subject justice while remaining within the prescribed space parameters, this chapter will offer an overview of the subject matter. Beginning with an examination of the general environment in which the Polish Jews functioned, it will then consider Polish-Jewish relations during the several chronological subperiods normally accepted by historians. Although a certain amount of brevity and, perhaps, even superficiality will no doubt result from this approach, the reader desiring further information or in-depth elaboration on the issues discussed herein will be referred to accessible published materials that will assist in filling the gaps in coverage.

A number of scholars have noted the various circumstances and forces whose unfortunate confluence in the two decades between the world wars produced such a bleak situation for the Jews of East Central Europe, especially Poland; hence, they can be summarized here.[1] One was the tremendous surge of patriotic enthusiasm released by the establishment of independent countries following World War I. This sense of national pride in liberation from hated foreign domination all too often evolved into a form of ethnoreligious chauvinism in which the numerically preponderant majority viewed the new state—with its administrative apparatus—as belonging solely to the "master nation." In turn, the majority could (and often did) employ the power of this apparatus to enforce its will and advance its group interests over those of fellow citizens who belonged to different ethnoreligious groupings. In short, as Roman Szporluk recently observed, the novel concept of the "state" as the ultimate weapon in the struggle of one nationality against the others within a polity—rather than being an arbitrator or mediator in this conflict—prevailed in most East European lands, including Poland.[2] When the population's lack of experience in macro- as well as micropolitics is taken into account, it becomes apparent why it was believed that political extremism, joined with a conviction that the sheer power of the newly won sovereignty alone, could suffice to solve the bewildering array of pressing social and economic problems confronting the infant states. This belief produced an atmosphere in which those without a firm grip on the organs of administrative control were at the mercy of the majority. The steady drift toward an authoritarian form of government tended to exacerbate this situation. Indeed, as Hugh Seton-Watson has noted, this tendency toward the growth and triumph of political ideologies "hostile to liberalism" had a particularly direct impact on the Jews, since "in so far as liberal ideas tend to go with equal treatment of the Jews, illiberal ideas go with repression of the Jews."[3]

The atmosphere of growing political intensity developed against a broad background of serious socioeconomic deficiencies that would have frustrated even the most enlightened, progressive, and experienced political leaders. Except for the Czech lands, Eastern Europe was an economically and socially underdeveloped region that did not make noteworthy strides during the interwar period. Most of the inhabitants were peasants, who tended to view the small proportion of urban dwellers as foreigners hostile to their traditional values and interests—a feeling shared by the gentry-derived intelligentsia and managerial elite. Industry was limited and often retarded in terms of technology and processes, and commerce was usually perceived as being dominated by minorities. The historic ruling circles of landowning nobility and clergy still wielded considerable power, although increasingly they had to share it with the emerging middle class of businessmen. As noted earlier, these groups often sought to substitute the authority of centralized state power in the form of protective tariffs, monopolies, wage and price controls, etc., for the meaningful agrarian and other reforms that would have placed their economies and societies on a sound, modern footing. The Great Depression underscored and accentuated these weaknesses, and the result was a series of economies that generally stagnated throughout this era. Finally, most of these states were multinational in composition, i.e., they possessed substantial ethnoreligious minorities; approximately one third of Poland's population consisted of East Slavic, German, Lithuanian, and, of course, Jewish inhabitants. Since many of these minority groups perceived the central government and its local equivalents (correctly, in most cases) as lethal weapons for their ethnoreligious emasculation by the ruling majority, their determined resistance to the government was a consistent, and frequently inflammatory, ingredient of the political scene. When one considers that the usual safety valve of emigration was closed by new restrictions imposed by the United States and other Western "recipient" lands, the potential for continual socioeconomic tension was dangerously high.

This was the environment within which the Polish Jews functioned. Accounting for 10 to 12 percent of the population at any given time, depending upon which figures are used, the Jews tended to concentrate occupationally in commerce, the various skilled crafts, and "free professions," although there were Jewish blue-collar and white-collar workers, farmers, and industrial capitalists as well. They were primarily a city people, comprising nearly one-third of Poland's urban population and over one-half in the backward eastern provinces of Volhynia and Polesie.[4] Renowned historian Ezra Mendelsohn observes that, occupationally, "in general, the Jewish population in interwar Poland may be termed lower middle class and proletarian, with a numerically small but important intelligentsia and wealthy bourgeoisie."[5] He also describes a typology of Eastern European Jewish community that applies to Poland.[6] In addition to those noted above, this type possessed the following characteristics: a relatively low level of assimilation or acculturation, continued adherence to religious orthodoxy and use of the Yiddish language, high birthrate and low rate of intermarriage, and an uneasy coexistence within the community of two forms of Jewish identity—orthodox religious, and secular national.[7] Their distinctive profile, major differences from the majority population, and the overall climate of interwar Poland made the Jews attractive targets for those elements of the Polish community who, for either doctrinaire or practical reasons, chose to focus their hostility on the Jewish minority. It is hard to quarrel with the conclusion that, whereas "generally Jews have flourished in lands of cultural and religious tolerance, political liberalism, stability, and economic growth," in Poland and most of Eastern Europe they found instead "chauvinism and intolerance, instability, economic stagnation, and extreme right-wing politics."[8]

The political dimension of the interwar Polish-Jewish relationship has received the most attention from scholars. It can be best appreciated by focusing on two separate but interconnected levels of Polish attitudes. One involves the position of individual political parties and movements or interest groups on the "Jewish Question" as displayed in formalized fashion, the other considers the stance of the Polish government as evinced in specific statutory, administrative, or programmatic acts that affected, directly or indirectly, the Jewish population. Certainly, there was a definite link between the two levels, as certain groups in the polity sought to give concrete legal expression to their theories. Since the posture of parties and the government evolved with, and reflected, the changing political, economic, and social climate of interwar Poland, it is instructive to view both within a chronological framework.

A brief examination of the positions on the "Jewish Question" advanced by the major political groups at the outset of Poland's independent existence will prove beneficial as a background to understanding the developments of the 1918–1926 period of "parliamentary democracy." Not surprisingly, most of those Poles opposed to according the Jews an equal role in the polity came from representatives of the nationalist right wing. Chief among them was the National Democratic, or *Endek* (from the acronym of its Polish name, Narodowa Demokracja) movement. This group centered much of its program and subsequent organizational activities on a strongly anti-Jewish platform. Founded before World War I under the aegis of Roman Dmowski, the National Democrats developed an ideologically based, formalized anti-Semitism that proved very attractive to increasing numbers of Poles as the years passed.[9] Briefly stated, this viewpoint featured two key ideas: most Jews were enemies of a resurrected independent Poland ruled by the "master" Polish nation, and those Jews who were favorable to the restoration neither could nor would ever be assimilated into the majority, no matter how much they might desire to. Thus, the only solution to the "Jewish Question" acceptable to the *Endeks* was a combination of a long-term program aiming at the eventual elimination of the Jews from Poland through a major drive to transfer them elsewhere in the world, especially Palestine, and a short-term plan to weaken the Jews economically, culturally, and politically as much as possible.[10] The only difference of opinion within *Endek* ranks was over how to accomplish these ends. Those party leaders of the older generation advocated the use of such measures as a mass economic boycott and the imposition of government restrictions on economic and cultural functions to force the Jews out of public life and, eventually, the country, whereas younger Nationalists preferred open violence in the form of beatings, property destruction, and other forms of often sadistic brutality directed against the Jews. Among other movements that endorsed the *Endek* perspective were the Christian Democrats of Wojciech Korfanty, the National Workers Party, and the small but influential group of landowning aristocrats organized into the Conservative Party.[11] Since the Nationalists, together with their allies, were the dominant political force in Poland prior to 1926, and exerted an increasingly strong ideological influence on the government after that, they defined the position that largely became that of the Polish state.

The most outspoken opposition to this stance came from the Polish Socialist Party (PPS). The party program adopted in 1919 at its Seventeenth Congress called for the guarantee of "full rights regardless of sex, religion, or nationality" to all citizens, and the granting of territorial self-government to those minorities "living in compact masses in certain parts of Poland."[12] The party went even further at its Nineteenth Congress in 1923, when it demanded the constitutional guarantee of minority language rights in public schools, the granting of state subsidies "without regard to national or religious interests," equal employment opportunities in the Polish civil service, and the end to "administrative persecution of the minorities."[13] At the same time, the Socialists opposed all proposals for conferring secular national (as opposed to religious) autonomy on the country's Jews. Although formal programmatic statements never addressed this issue directly, PPS legislators—especially the Jewish ones—argued the traditional Marxist attitude of secularization and assimilation with the non-Jewish population as the only viable way in which the Jews and society as a whole could progress from the medieval "feudal" situation symbolized by the "ghetto." Hence the Jews should secularize and polonize as quickly as possible, and the Poles should take measures to stimulate rather than retard this development.[14]

The final segment of the Polish political spectrum to consider involves the peasant movement. The partition period bequeathed independent Poland several separate peasant parties, and their numbers increased during the initial postwar decade as a result of internal factionalism. The two most important, in terms of size and influence, were the Piast and Wyzwolenie, which differed rather markedly in their views of the "Jewish Question." Perhaps because it was ideologically and, in some cases, personally close to the Socialists, the latter was far more tolerant and enlightened in both word and deed. The initial Wyzwolenie program statement before the newly elected Constituent Assembly in July 1919 committed it to working for the assurance of "absolute freedom" to other religions despite recognizing that Roman Catholicism was the faith of the majority of inhabitants.[15] Two years later, the party adopted a program platform that was more specific.[16] Article 3 demanded complete freedom for the minorities to develop their own distinctive cultures and to use their own languages in educational, administrative, and judicial settings, as well as the granting of territorial autonomy where concentration of a minority warranted it. Article 13 dealt with civil and legal rights. After affirming that the party considered "the safeguarding of the rights of man and the citizen" as one of its "most pressing tasks," Wyzwolenie insisted that no citizen could be deprived of his/her rights for reasons of one's social standing, religion, or nationality, whether this deprivation is the result of law or the customs of privilege enjoyed by another social class, religion, or nationality." At the same time, the party urged the rapid development of credit as well as commercial cooperatives for small peasant farmers. An expanded version of this program accepted in 1925 reaffirmed the Wyzwolenie dedication to these principles, which were also professed by several smaller peasant parties.[17]

The other major agrarian party, the Piast, from the outset assumed a more hostile attitude toward the national minorities, including the Jews. Initially its program firmly stated the conviction that "freedom of religion and conviction" would have to be assured in the new state, a position reaffirmed by its president and three-time premier, Wincenty Witos, in a speech before the Constituent Assembly in July 1919.[18] This attitude changed abruptly under the stress of the Polish-Soviet war, during which Witos served as premier. His memoirs reveal a strong animosity toward the Jews even before the outbreak of fighting, which the conflict brought into the open.[19] The party's press organ, *Piast*, regularly featured articles and editorials denouncing Jewish conduct for disloyalty to Poland during the war, with Witos himself penning some of the more overtly anti-Jewish pieces even after hostilities had ceased.[20] Not surprisingly, this outlook found expression in the revised party program adopted in 1921.[21] Although it stated the Piast desire to live with the minorities "according to the principles of justice and harmonious cooperation" and pledged the party to work for the "statutory guarantee of full and free development of their cultural and national life," the program contained several qualifying provisions. It announced the party's wish "to apply Christian principles in private, social, and state life," and demanded that the cities "become vital centers of Polish national culture and Polish economic life"; it also called for the establishment of cooperatives as the best way to develop trade "in a direction meeting the interests of the people." The Piast party completed its apparent shift to the anti-Semitic Right by signing the overtly antiminority Lanckoronski Pact with the National Democrats and Christian Democrats in May 1923. Among other things, this agreement pledged the signatories to work for Polish ethnic and Roman Catholic religious predominance in every facet of national life, and specifically called for a *numerus clausus* in education and government jobs and contracts.[22]

Given the fact that the Nationalists and their allies dominated domestic politics during the first era of Polish independence, it was inevitable that Polish Jews would face a very difficult situation. Actual descriptions and enumerations of specific events in the anti-Jewish campaign have appeared elsewhere, and need not be detailed here.[23] The Jews suffered a series of pogroms in the immediate postwar years, bore the brunt of blame for the imposition of the Minorities Protection Treaty on Poland by the Great Powers, and incurred the wrath of the Right for the election of Gabriel Narutowicz as the first president of independent Poland—who paid for this "Jewish support" with his life. With the final cessation of border hostilities in 1921, overt anti-Jewish excesses gave way to a more systematic drive to undermine the Jewish economic position, in keeping with the basic National Democratic strategy on this issue.[24] Those Jews holding jobs in the prewar Austrian civil service were "retired early," and replaced with Poles; Jews became virtually nonexistent in municipal, as well as national, bureaucracies, and were very rare in public education (as both teachers and, in universities, students), the officer corps (except as doctors), and various other state enterprises. Jewish businessmen very seldom secured loans from state credit institutions, and Jewish artisans and professionals obtained occupational licenses only with great difficulty (and, frequently, through bribery). Changes in taxation policy under the guise of "tax reform" hit small Jewish entrepreneurs particularly hard. Perhaps the gravest blow to Jewish economic interests, and the one most indicative of the official sanction behind the anti-Semitic drive, was the law passed in 1919 prohibiting any labor or commercial activities on Sunday. Since most Jewish businesses observed their Sabbath day of rest on Saturday but opened on Sundays to a substantial Christian trade, this measure effectively closed their establishments two days of the week, while competing Christian firms were open six days. Although subsequently amended to exclude certain categories of business activity, the law remained in effect and dealt many Jews a severe economic setback.

There were other government measures directed against Jews. A 1920 law defining the eligibility for Polish citizenship for those residing on Polish territory before the war appeared innocuous on the surface, but was used as a pretext for attempts to deport thousands of Russian and Lithuanian Jews who earlier had fled to Poland to escape tsarist persecution. The electoral law for the Sejm (parliament) made it especially difficult for Jews and other territorially dispersed minorities to send their representatives to the lower chamber of parliament. When challenged on these and other clearly discriminatory measures, Polish officials could always point to their acceptance of the

Minorities Protection Treaty and the constitutional guarantees of religious and ethnic freedom as proof of their good will and intentions.

Faced with these harsh realities, the Polish Jews tried a variety of defensive strategies, none of which really worked.[25] In part, this failure was due to the fragmented nature of Jewish politics and the inability to mount a unified, coherent response that might have diminished some of the government's enthusiasm for pursuing anti-Semitic policies. The most visible Jewish tactic in the initial postwar stage was the formation of a coalition of some parties representing the other major national minorities in order to contest the 1922 parliamentary elections and, they hoped, to function as a potent force within the new legislature. Under the driving force of Yitshak Grünbaum, leader of the General Zionists of Congress Poland, the "Bloc of National Minorities" did, in fact, enjoy some success in the balloting. but it was symptomatic of the Jewish political scene that many Jews, including fellow Zionists, did not back the bloc. The Zionists of Galicia wanted to pursue an accommodation with the government, in which each side would leave the other alone and live in relative harmony, while the anti-Zionist Orthodox party, Agudath Yisroel, favored a policy of active cooperation with and support for the regime, rather than merely coexisting with it.[26] Finally, the Jewish Socialist party (known generally as the Bund) sought a total reconstruction of society, economy, and polity in which capitalism would yield to socialism, and anti-Semitism would likewise disappear; to achieve this end and protect Jewish interests in the interim, the Bund advocated a working partnership with the Polish Left.[27] There were other Jewish movements as well, but their political influence was negligible compared to these four.[28]

During this initial phase of interwar Polish history, the General Zionists and their Galician rivals dominated the Jewish political scene. The minorities bloc tried to assert its presence in parliament, but made little lasting impact beyond offering a method of exerting public pressure on the successive Right-Center governments in (mostly fruitless) attempts to thwart their anti-Jewish and antiminority plans. But as the intensity of anti-Semitism began to abate in the mid-1920s, while simultaneously the Polish state realized its desperate need for substantial Western financial aid to put the economy on a solid footing, the mood in both camps swung in favor of some kind of positive working relationship. The two eminent Galician Zionists, Leon Reich and Osias Thon, assumed leadership of the Jewish Club in the Sejm, and economic reformer Władysław Grabski became premier, as well as minister of finance in the cabinet. Negotiations opened between the two sides, and culminated in the signing of an accord in July 1925.[29]

This so-called *Ugoda* consisted of forty-two points, of which only the first twelve were ever officially acknowledged by the Poles.[30] On the surface, it seemed like a major advance for Polish Jewry. Their leaders agreed to support the "inviolability" of Poland's frontiers and her foreign policy, and to strive for "internal consolidation" within the country—a provision interpreted as being repudiation of cooperation with the other ethnoreligious minorities in alliance against the government.[31] For its part, the Polish leadership promised, among other things, to approve reform of the governing Jewish communal bodies (*kehilloth*) in Galicia and the eastern border territories, facilitate the observation of religious restrictions and duties in public schools and the armed forces, and provide official recognition—and consequent eligibility for public funding—for Jewish schools. But even as it was being announced, the *Ugoda* was vilified from both Polish and Jewish quarters—the former denouncing it as a "sellout" of basic Polish interests to a hostile, harmful group within the polity, the latter condemning Reich and Thon for assuring an anti-Semitic regime of Jewish international, as well as domestic, backing in return for a group of vague promises that did not address the real problems of Polish Jewry and had no mechanism to ensure their fulfillment.

Major political developments soon rendered moot the question of whether the Grabski government had acted in good faith or cynically exploited the naive Jews for foreign policy reasons. On May 12, 1926, Marshal Józef Piłsudski staged a successful coup d'état against a newly formed Center-Right government headed by Witos. Piłsudski, who had withdrawn from overt political life in 1923 rather than accept the dominance of his nationalist rivals, seemed an ideal figure to end the problems facing Poland's Jews. By 1926, he was avowedly nonpartisan, yet with a leftist past that appeared to preclude any overt anti-Semitism and simultaneously assure the hostility of the Right and Center. Moreover, he was clearly a strong personality who promised a government based on order and stability to replace the political and economic chaos that had plagued the country since 1918, and

produce an environment conducive to the positive development of
Polish Jewry. Other groups on the Left and among the minorities
shared this perception, and the time appeared ripe for an actual
working partnership between the Jews and their government.[32]

This brought Agudath Yisroel to the fore among Jewish
political leadership. The two sides had much to gain from
harmonious interaction. Piłsudski could acquire Jewish support
for his *Sanacja* regime against his opponents on the Right, Center,
and even the Left, while the Agudath could neutralize its
Zionist, secularist, and other rivals for supremacy in Jewish
politics. Moreover, the styles of each seemed well suited to the
other. The Agudath desired to work with executive and
administrative authorities to advance Jewish interests while
publicly backing government policies and programs. For his part,
Piłsudski preferred his Jewish partner to be a religious group
concerned with obtaining specific concessions rather than a
secular party pressing for broad political demands. As an added
bonus, Piłsudski would gain access to the Agudath voting power in
the cities of the Congress Poland area, and reap considerable good
will abroad.

Initially, this relationship of mutual exploitation appeared
to function advantageously for both parties. The hostile
atmosphere that had fostered a widespread anti-Jewish
movement largely disappeared, as did attacks on Jewish
property and individuals. The Agudath leadership publicly
voiced its endorsement of *Sanacja* policies at every opportunity,
and offered tangible proof of its commitment to the arrangement
by backing Jewish participation in the 1928 and 1930
parliamentary elections on the officially sponsored "Nonpartisan Bloc for Cooperation with the Government" (BBWR)
list, rather than running a separate Jewish slate. In return, the
regime utilized administrative measures to promote Agudath
interests in the two important areas of Jewish education and the
*kehilloth*, where the orthodox movement gained ground at the
expense of the secularists.[33] As the economy began to bring some
relative prosperity to Poland and some of her citizens, the
Agudath approach seemed to be justified.

Yet, all was not as favorable as surface appearances would
indicate. The Agudath deputies remained a minority in the
Jewish Parliamentary Club, and could not prevent other members
of the group from strongly criticizing the *Sanacja* on the national
budget, and voting against it on such key issues as amending the

constitution and granting the government extraordinary powers.[34] To compound these legislative difficulties, Jewish representation in the parliament diminished dramatically despite the Agudath's enthusiastic participation on the government ticket in the 1928 and 1930 contests.[35] In turn, these developments stimulated Grünbaum to revive his idea of a minorities bloc to pressure the government into providing better treatment for its non-Polish citizens, and the Jewish Left became increasingly vocal in advocating the belief that only a strong alliance with its Polish counterparts could help the Jews. Even more unsettling was the behavior of the government itself. Public statements to the contrary, the state began to default on its public and private assurances of assistance to the Jewish population. It failed to provide adequate funding for Jewish religious education, repeal the compulsory Sunday rest law, and end the employment discrimination against Jews in the public sector. Despite executive orders prohibiting it, the *numerus clausus* continued to be applied in higher education. Furthermore, in part because of the rapprochement that Piłsudski struck with the large landowners (usually associated with his presence at an October 1926 meeting with conservative nobility at the Nieśwież of Prince Janusz Radziwiłł, the regime abandoned work on the much-needed reforms of the unfair tax and agrarian structures. These failures to act resulted in an ever increasing tax burden on the urban Jewish population, and a growing sense of frustrated wrath among the land-starved peasantry, whose ire could be easily redirected away from the landlords and to the local Jewish shopkeepers and moneylenders.

The Great Depression, which hit Poland harder and lasted longer than in most other countries, was particularly devastating for the Jews. Numerous small businesses failed in the normal course of events, and the policy adopted by the government to halt and reverse the economic collapse furthered this process. The regime opted for a program of étatism that, while not demonstrably motivated by anti-Semitic considerations, nonetheless effectively wiped out Jewish commercial, financial, and artisan establishments by taxing them into oblivion and regulating to a near standstill those that did survive.[36] Employment of Jews in the national and local bureaucracies and nationalized corporations, already very low, became virtually nonexistent, and budget reductions nearly eliminated whatever state services and funds had been available to the Jewish population. Perhaps more ominous for the latter was the tide of popular anti-Semitism that began to swell rapidly in the early 1930s. That the National Democrats launched a major campaign to blame the Jews for all of Poland's political and social, as well as economic, ills should come as no surprise; indeed, after charging the *Sanacja* with drawing its chief support from the Jews, a leading *Endek* politician observed in July 1931 that "Polish public opinion representing all social segments will turn against the Jews, and this will be solely the result of their own policies."[37]

The reaction among those Poles not as committed to anti-Semitism as a basic element of their program seemed to validate this observation, and provided a grim harbinger of things to come. This was especially true of the peasantry. When the three main peasant parties finally set aside their bickering and merged to form a single Peasant Party (Stronnictwo Ludowe) in March 1931, its new program made no separate mention of the Jews, apart from repeating the earlier Piast observation that the cities had to become "vital centers of Polish culture and economic life." Simultaneously, the movement reaffirmed its devotion to complete religious, civil, economic, and political rights for all minorities, and condemned "all lawlessness and oppression"— provided that the non-Poles "honestly fulfilled their obligations to the state."[38] But within two years, the Polish peasants were displaying evidence that the ceaseless *Endek* hammering away at the Jews as the source of Poland's evils was bearing fruit among the rural masses. In 1933, the Institute of Social Economics (Instytut Gospodarstwa Społecznego), what today might be termed a "liberal think tank," conducted a survey to gather personal testimonies from peasants regarding their past experiences and present circumstances in depression-wracked Poland. The first volume of selected "memoires" revealed overt anti-Semitism in nearly one-fourth of the peasants surveyed.[39] Although verbal nuances varied according to the individual authors, the general viewpoint expressed was consistent on certain points: the Jew was a parasitic middleman who exploited the naive, ignorant peasants by paying below-market prices for farm products and then charging exorbitant ones for manufactured goods or essential raw materials; the Jew was an archetypal "loan shark" who deceived the peasantry into overextending their credit at usurious rates, then foreclosing on their land; the Jew was responsible for using his influence abroad to knock the bottom out of the international market for Polish agricultural products. The second volume contained fewer peasant contributions, but over one-half of them expressed anti-Jewish feelings to some extent.[40]

The rising contagion of anti-Semitism coincided with, and was somewhat stimulated by, events in both the international and domestic arenas. The coming of Adolf Hitler to power in Germany in January 1933 soon offered concrete examples of how a determined regime could persecute its Jewish population without fear of serious repercussion. In September of the following year, Polish foreign minister Józef Beck announced that his government no longer felt bound by the terms of the Minorities Protection Treaty, and henceforth would view the situation of its national minorities as a purely internal problem. Developments within Poland began to run parallel to those outside the country. The years 1933–1935 were marked by a perceptible rise in organized anti-Semitic activity, some of it quite violent, along with nationalist attempts to force the government into enacting formal legal restrictions on the Jews. The Roman Catholic church leadership offered little relief to the increasingly beleaguered Jews. When a delegation of rabbis visited August Cardinal Hlond, primate of Poland, in June 1934 to request his assistance in discouraging anti-Jewish excesses, he responded by issuing a pastoral letter condemning violence and disorder. However, he accused the Jews of bringing these difficulties upon themselves through a variety of offenses against Christian sensibilities, including the distribution of pornography and the financing of communist agitation in Poland.[41] To compound matters, the *Sanacja* camp became preoccupied with the steadily deteriorating health of Piłsudski, and its efforts to push a new, authoritarian constitution through parliament. Consequently, it did not act as determinedly as it might have to counter the various anti-Semitic pressures.

The death of Piłsudski in May 1935 opened the final gloomy chapter in the history of interwar Polish Jewry.[42] As long as Piłsudski had controlled the state apparatus, his enormous personal authority had prevented the government from assuming an explicitly anti-Semitic position. But his successors, bereft of genuine legitimacy and seeking support and credibility from the Center and Right of the opposition, began to adopt the authoritarianism and ethnoreligious chauvinism of the latter. This included—and, at times, seemed to center on—an overt anti-

Jewish crusade that stopped short of condoning actual physical violence, but appeared committed to nearly every other type of assault against Jewish interests. Premier Felicjan Sławoj-Składkowski himself, in his infamous *owszem* ("of course") speech to the Sejm in June 1936, launched an economic boycott of Jewish establishments that soon reached epidemic proportions. Legislators affiliated with the regime introduced various bills proposing anti-Jewish legislation, of which one—designed to restrict severely the practice of Jewish ritual slaughter—actually became law in 1936.

When the *Sanacja* introduced a new government support organization—the Camp of National Unity, or OZN—in February 1937 with a determined anti-Semitic posture, the atmosphere became even more threatening for the Jews. The Roman Catholic hierarchy enthusiastically endorsed this trend, and a wave of organized violence directed against Jewish persons and property swept the country with increased intensity.[43] The authorities were strangely unable to apprehend those responsible, nor did they attempt to prevent nationalist youth from hounding Jewish students out of the universities, especially from such key professional schools as medicine, engineering, and law. Furthermore, despite the crucial shortage of trained practitioners in these fields, the government accepted the decisions of the relevant professional associations to exclude Jews from their rolls.[44] Finally, while publicly decrying their country's unfortunate lot in having so many Jews, the regime tirelessly pursued various possibilities of securing locales where Polish Jews could emigrate without any limiting quotas—including the French colony of Madagascar.[45] Indeed, in the period from 1936 to 1939, the Polish authorities became among the most fervent Zionists in the world! While perhaps disputing the contemporary observation that in 1939 the National Democratic Party was the "strongest, best organized, and most vital" opposition force in the country, one cannot deny the subsequent assertion that its anti-Semitic propaganda "has served to so magnify the Jewish problem in Poland, which calls for immediate and drastic solution," that it appears far more pressing to the survival of the Polish state than "the much more vital problem of the five million Ukrainians and the one million Germans."[46]

The response encountered from the Polish community proved interesting. Those already committed to anti-Semitism as a cornerstone of their political or socioeconomic programs were predictably pleased, although desirous of pushing the government even further in this direction. Conversely, some intellectuals and former close followers of Piłsudski of a liberal persuasion decried this shift in policy. In late 1937, they formed the Democratic Club, later renamed the Democratic Party (Klub Demokratyczny, Stronnictwo Demokratyczne), which worked actively to combat nationalist chauvinism in general and anti-Semitism in particular. Although not a major factor on the political scene, the Democratic Party, in the words of a contemporary Jewish commentator, contained "some of the noblest minds and hearts in Poland" whose voices had been "stilled and subdued by the violent anti-Jewish propaganda" but "cannot and will not remain silent forever."[47] But there were also some surprising reactions among Polish groups, especially the Socialists and peasants. The former, normally solidly against any form of ethnoreligious chauvinism, as an organization continued to condemn these latest trends and to assist Jews whenever possible. Nonetheless, a special pamphlet written by a leading socialist ideologue entitled *The Jewish Question and Socialism* noted that only those Jews thoroughly assimilated would have a future in a socialist, democratic Poland; the overwhelming majority would have to emigrate elsewhere.[48] Even though this one publication by no means signified a change in the official party position, its very appearance indicated the extent to which anti- Jewish propaganda had convinced even some Socialists that most Jews were indeed aliens, and had to leave Poland for the well-being of all concerned.

Perhaps the reaction of the Peasant Party was the most striking of all. In December 1935, in the midst of the anti-Semitic fervor then sweeping the land, the party advanced a revised program that directly addressed the "Jewish Question" for the first time.[49] After reaffirming their commitment to "equality before the law" to all citizens "irrespective of their nationality and religion," article 7 declared that the Jews were more populous in Poland than elsewhere in Europe and, since they could not be assimilated, formed "a consciously alien nation in Poland" that retarded the growth of an ethnically Polish middle class. Hence, through the devices of economic boycott, cooperatives, and the support of Jewish emigration "by all available means," the transfer of commercial and financial functions controlled by Jews into Polish hands would be accomplished—"as the most vital interests of the Polish state and nation demand." The party did decry "fruitless acts of violence" against the Jews, but left no doubt as to its intent. But even as some younger activists affiliated with the party youth group Wici were warning against any cooperation with the nationalists as a movement "decidedly hostile" to the peasantry, the main leadership was rethinking its position.[50] Resolutions passed at the next congress in January 1937 completely omitted mention of the Jews, and six months later the central party press organ dismissed the regime's growing anti-Semitism as a transparent device to prolong Poland's real evil, "the gentry exploitation of the peasants."[51] Except for continued emphasis on the need for the expansion of a cooperative system, subsequent public pronouncements and internally circulated documents—including letters from the exiled Witos— avoided discussion of the "Jewish Question." For the peasantry, the real enemy was the increasingly totalitarian regime, and not the Jew—the real need was for a true agrarian restructuring and political reform; driving the Jews out of Poland was of distinctly secondary importance.

In the face of this general hostility and concerted anti-Jewish activity, there was little effective response available to the Jews. With the Zionist and Agudath strategies no longer viable, two movements on the extreme wings of Jewish politics attempted to fill the resulting void. One was the Bund, which hoped that a sound relationship with the Polish Left could overcome the official anti-Semitic drive. But apart from a few victories in municipal elections and special "self-defense" squads of its members who successfully protected Jews from violence in some areas, the Bund did little to ease the mounting pressure on Polish Jewry.[52] The other was the "revisionist" wing of Zionism, which was far more militant politically and conservative in a socioeconomic sense than earlier Zionism had been.[53] Under the forceful leadership of Vladimir Jabotinsky, and with the enthusiastic support of the Polish government, the Revisionists tried to launch a major "evacuation" campaign of Jews from Poland and other Eastern European lands to Palestine. With Great Britain shutting off any further immigration to that land in the late 1930s, however, this effort at rescuing Polish Jews from what increasingly promised to be a sad fate likewise failed.

The above narrative, sketchy though it is, leads to several conclusions. First, it is clear that both interwar Poland and her

Jewish population were undergoing a major socioeconomic transformation. Originally, the Jews were what Joseph Rothschild has termed a "pariah" minority, an ethnoreligious group distinct from the majority and "performing commercial and entrepreneurial functions that are conspicuous, remunerative, important, yet socially disparaged in a setting where the host society consists of warrior nobles who disdain, and of peasants who lack the resources for, these entrepreneurial activities."[54] But by 1918, Poland was already evolving away from the type of socioeconomic structure that provided the necessary precondition for the continued existence of the "pariah" minority as a substratum tolerated by the majority.

Political pressures unique to the period and this part of the world hastened the process. From the outset Poland, like nearly all other new nation-states in Eastern Europe, was beset by monumental international and domestic problems, and had only nationalism as a major unifying factor. Since the exclusive nature of this force precluded sharing the government with citizens not members of the Polish nation as defined ethnically, the state became a weapon in the struggle to assure majority dominance over the minority. Simultaneously, as the evolving economy pushed ever more Poles into direct competition with Jews for the limited resources and markets available, it was inevitable that the state apparatus would become attractive as a major tool for modernizing society and expanding the economy on behalf of the Poles and at the expense of the Jews. Of course, the refusal of the vested interests in the polity to adopt the kind of extensive economic reforms that would have benefited all citizens further contributed to the difficult position of the Jews, who thus served as convenient distractions from the pressing needs of the country—as, in fact, the Peasant Party pointed out. Add to these factors the long-standing tradition of anti-Semitism in Poland's main religion—Roman Catholicism— and it is hardly surprising that this movement would gain in strength throughout the two decades. It is hard to quarrel with Mendelsohn's judgment that "the combination of traditional hatred of Jews, the triumph of nationalism, internal weakness, and the role of the Jewish Question in the struggle for power between the moderate right and the extreme right" all laid the foundation for the ultimate disaster of Polish Jewry.[55]

There are several points involving the Jews themselves that remain to be considered before leaving this subject. One was their inability to coalesce around one leader or leadership and thus present a united front to the Poles. Of course, given what appears to be the congenital political divisiveness in Poland among Poles as well as non-Poles, this may simply have been a function of the general political environment. No doubt, the changes within the Polish Jewish community, which possessed religious as well as secular political dimensions, also contributed to this fragmentation. Whatever the reasons, the resulting disunity seriously weakened Jewish opposition to organized anti-Semitism. Another point involves the undeniable fact that, whereas interwar Poland did not offer a very positive setting for individual Jews to prosper, it did provide favorable conditions for a blossoming of Jewish culture, both religious and secular. True, the absence of state funding did not help Jewish scholarship, music, art, dance, drama, and literature—let alone religious studies—to develop. Nevertheless, neither did what became an increasingly official anti-Semitism seriously impede that development. Thus, while interwar Poland may have been bad for Jews per se, on the whole it was not so bad, and perhaps in some instances it was even good, for Judaism. Unfortunately for them and the world, the Polish Jews and their many accomplishments were virtually wiped from the face of the earth by the Holocaust.

## Notes

The author would like to thank the libraries and their staffs at the University of Illinois-Urbana and Indiana University-Bloomington, together with the Russian and East European Institute of Indiana University and the Center for Russian and East European Studies of the University of Illinois-Urbana, for their generous financial and personnel assistance in pursuing the research for this paper.

1. Among those works most lucidly describing and analyzing these conditions are S. Ettinger, "Jews and Non-Jews in East and Central Europe between the Wars: An Outline," in B. Vago and G. Mosse, eds. *Jews and Non-Jews in Eastern Europe, 1918–1945* (New York, 1974) 1–19; E. Mendelsohn, *The Jews of East Central Europe Between the World Wars* (Bloomington, Ind., 1983) 1–23; and J. Lestchinsky, "The Industrial and Social Structure of the Jewish Population of Interbellum Poland," *YIVO Annual of Jewish Social Science*, 11 (1956/57): 243–246.

2. Szporluk advances this thesis in an article focused on Czechoslovakia, "War by Other Means," *Slavic Review*, 44 (1985): 1, 20–26, and elaborated upon it as it related to Poland in his paper, "State

and Nation in Polish Political Thought," presented at an international conference on "Poland Between the Wars" (Indiana University-Bloomington, 1985).

3. H. Seton-Watson, "Government Policies Towards the Jews in Pre-Communist Eastern Europe," *Bulletin on Soviet and East European Jewish Affairs*, 4 (1969): 21.

4. There are numerous detailed discussions of the socioeconomic and demographic structure of Polish Jewry available for the researcher. In addition to the above cited article by Lestchinsky, see also his "The Jews in the Cities of the Republic of Poland," *YIVO Annual of Jewish Social Science*, 1 (1946): 156–177 for the perceptions of a contemporary Jewish scholar; more recent examinations of this question include the books by S. Bronsztejn, *Ludność zydowska w Polsce w okresie miedzywojennym* (Warsaw, 1963); and J. Marcus, *Social and Political History of the Jews in Poland*, 1919–1939 (New York, 1983), especially 27–258; and the chapter by G. Castellan, "Remarks on the Social Structure of the Jewish Community in Poland between the Two World Wars," in Vago and Mosse, *Jews and Non-Jews*, 187–201. For more specialized studies, see R. Mahler, "Jews in Public Service and the Liberal Professions in Poland, 1918–1939," *Jewish Social Studies*, 6 (1944): 291–349; and the two articles by J. Tomaszewski, "Robotnicy żydowscy w Polsce w latach 1921–1939 (szkic statystyczny)," *Biuletyn Żydowskiego Instytutu Historycznego*, 51 (1964): 21–39, and "Robotnicy zydowscy w Warszawie międzywojennej (uwagi statystyczne)," ibid., 81 (1972): 71–84.

5. Mendelsohn, *Jews of East Central Europe*, 27.

6. Ibid., 6–7.

7. The best examinations of the Jewish dilemma regarding acculturation and assimilation in Poland are by C. S. Heller, "Assimilation: A Deviant Pattern Among the Jews of Interwar Poland," *The Jewish Journal of Sociology*, 15, no. 2 (December 1973): 221–237, and "Poles of Jewish Background—The Case of Assimilation Without Integration in Interwar Poland," in J. Fishman, ed., *Studies on Polish Jewry 1919–1939* (New York, 1974), 242–276.

8. Mendelsohn, *Jews of East Central Europe*, 5.

9. On the National Democrats, see the two books by J. J. Terej, *Idee, mity, realia: Szkice do dziejów Narodowej Demokracji* (Warsaw, 1971) and Rzeczywistość i polityka: Ze studiów nad dziejami najnowszymi Narodowej Demokracji (Warsaw, 1971); and two more works by R. Wapiński, Endecja na Pomorzu, 1920–1939 (Gdańsk, 1966) and *Narodowa Demokracja, 1893–1939* (Wrocław, 1980).

10. The best source of *Endek* views on the Jewish Question are the writings of Dmowski himself, especially his *Polityka polska i obudowanie państwa* (Warsaw, 1926), and *Myśli nowoczesnego Polaka*, 7th ed. (London, 1953). See also two biographical sketches, A. Micewski, *Roman Dmowski* (Warsaw, 1971), and I. Wolikowska, *Roman Dmowski: Czlowiek, Polak, Przyjaciel* (Chicago, 1961).

11. The Christian Democrats, organized during this period as the Christian National Labor Party, called for "the organization of the Polish state on Christian principles," and an increase in ethnic Polish involvement in trade and industry, although professing their belief in complete religious freedom for all citizens—A. Belcikowska, *Stronnictwa i związki polityczne w Polsce* (Warsaw, 1925), 124–129. On the Christian Democrats in general, see B. Krzywoblocka, *Chadecja, 1918–1937* (Warsaw, 1974), and the biography of their leader by M. Orzechowski, *Wojciech Korfanty: Biografia polityczna* (Wrocław, 1975); less objective is the article by W. Bitner, "O prawdziwe oblicze 'Partii katolickiej' w dwudziestoleciu," *Więź*, 62 (1963): 2, 110–112. The National Workers Party likewise endorsed a predominant position for Roman Catholicism while advocating equality for other religions and national and cultural autonomy for the minorities, but affirmed that "the preponderance of Jews in certain branches of trade and production is harmful," and should be replaced by "the Polish and Christian element." Bełcikowska, 315–319. On this party, see R. Wapinski, *Działalność Narodowej Partii Robotniczej na terenie województwa pomorskiego w latach 1920–1930* (Gdańsk, 1962), and the combined study of both parties by H. Przbylski, *Chrześcijańska Demokracja i Narowoda Partia Robotnicza w latach 1926–1937* (Warsaw, 1980). The Conservative Party was the most outspokenly hostile to the Jews, categorizing them as a "destructive force" intent on "harming Aryan societies" and driven by "hatred towards Christianity." Bełcikowska, 731. See the two fine studies of the Polish Conservative movement by S. Rudnicki, *Działalność polityczna polskich konserwatystów, 1918–1926* (Warsaw, 1980), and W. Wladyka, *Działalność polityczna polskich stronnictw konserwatywnych w latach 1926–1935* (Wrocław, 1977).

12. Bełcikowska, 362. For the PPS, see the books by J. Holzer, *PPS: Szkic dziejów* (Warsaw, 1977), and A. Tymieniecka, *Polityka Polskiej Partii Socjalistycznej w latach 1924–1928* (Warsaw, 1969).

13. Bełcikowska, *Stronnictwa i związki polityczne*, 370.

14. Historian Pawel Korzec has observed that, on the question of Jewish national autonomy, the socialist opposition "was more intransigent than the rightest groups"—"Antisemitism in Poland as an Intellectual, Social, and Political Movement," in Fishman, *Studies*, 36. The standard PPS position was articulated by the leading socialist spokesman on nationality affairs, Leon Wasilewski, in a book published during the war, *Die Judenfrage in Kongress-Polen* (Vienna, 1915); for the views of socialist leaders who themselves were Jewish and frequent proponents of this position in parliament, see H. Piasecki, "Hermann Diamond w okresie II Rzeczypospolitej (Maj 1926-Luty 1931)," *Biuletyn Żydowskiego Instytutu Historycznego*, 113 (1980): 44–45, and A. Leinwand, *Posel Herman Lieberman* (Wrocław, 1983).

15. "Deklaracja PSL-Wyzwolenie w sprawie stosunku do rządu, złożona przez Prezesa Stronnictwa na posiedzeniu Sejmu

Ustawodawczego (22 lipca 1919)," in S. Giza and S. Lato, eds., *Materialy żródłowe do historii ruchu ludowego*, 2 (Warsaw, 1967): 12–16. Hereafter cited as *MZHRL* 2.

16. Ibid., 49–57.

17. Ibid., 116–134, especially 119–120, 124, 133–134. Other peasant parties worth noting that echoed the Wyzwolenie line were the Independent Peasant Party (164–175), the "Left" (19–25), and the Radical Peasant Party (71–80). In the latter two cases, there were some interesting reservations attached to the call for ethnoreligious tolerance. The "Left" was willing to extend complete legal and civil equality to the minorities "to the extent that Poles enjoy them in the mother countries of those nationalities," (20), and the Independent Peasant Party, a Communist ally, likewise made its call for tolerance conditional on the minorities "not acting out any animosity in their relationship with the Republic" (77).

18. "Deklaracja PSL Piast w sprawach ogólnych, złożona przez Prezesa Stronnictwa...na posiedzeniu Sejmu Ustawodawczego (22 lipca 1919)," in *MZHRL* 2: 9–12. The program was adopted in June 1919, and is in ibid., 25–29.

19. W. Witos, *Moje wspomnienia*, 2 (Paris, 1964): 184–185, 307–308, 323–324, 391–392. An excellent biographical profile of Witos is by A. Zakrzewski, *Wincenty Witos: Chłopski polityk i mąż stanu* (Warsaw, 1977), which passes over his anti-Jewish sentiments.

20. For example, see his editorials "Żydzi a Polska" and "Jeszcze Żydzi a Polska" in *Piast* issues of October 9 and October 23, 1921.

21. *MZHRL* 2: 58–71.

22. Ibid., 80–92.

23. For example, the article by Korzec cited earlier ("Antisemitism in Poland") and his later book, *Juifs en Pologne: La question juive pendant l'entre-deux-guerres* (Paris, 1980); S. Segal, *The New Poland and the Jews* (New York, 1938); O. Janowsky, *People at Bay: The Jewish Problem in East Central Europe* (London, 1938); C. Heller, *On the Edge of Destruction: Jews of Poland Between the Two World Wars* (New York, 1977); and an excellent study of the background to and events of the immediate postwar period by F. Golczewski, *Polnisch-Jüdische Beziehungen, 1881–1922* (Wiesbaden, 1981).

24. For a comprehensive portrayal of economic anti-Semitism, see the contemporary work by W. Alter, *Antysemityzm gospodarczy w świetle cyfr* (Warsaw, 1937).

25. For concise information and penetrating analyses of Jewish politics during the interwar years, see the pieces by E. Mendelsohn, "The Dilemma of Jewish Politics in Poland: Four Responses," in Vago and Mosse, *Jews and Non-Jews*, 205–220, and J. Rothschild, "Ethnic Peripheries versus Ethnic Cores: Jewish Political Strategies in Interwar Poland," *Political Science Quarterly*, 96 (1981–1982), 4: 591–605.

26. An excellent study of Polish Zionism during this era is by E.

Mendelsohn, *Zionism in Poland: The Formative Years, 1915–1926* (New Haven, 1981). For Agudath Yisroel, see the article by the same author, "The Politics of Agudath Yisroel in Inter-War Poland," *Soviet Jewish Affairs*, 2 (1972), 2: 47–60; the doctoral dissertation by G. Bacon, *Agudath Israel in Poland, 1916–1939: An Orthodox Jewish Response to the Challenge of Modernity* (Ann Arbor, 1981), and the article by the same author, "Religious Solidarity Versus Class Interest: The Case of Poaley Agudat Yisreal in Poland, 1922–1939," *Soviet Jewish Affairs*, 13 (1983), 2: 49–62.

27. The best work available on the Bund in English remains B. Johnpoll, *The Politics of Futility: The General Jewish Workers Bund of Poland, 1917–1943* (Ithaca, N.Y., 1967).

28. Among these should be mentioned the Poale Zion, Mizrachi Zionist, Folkspartei, and the Zeire Zion.

29. For a history of these negotiations and a detailed discussion of the *Ugoda's* terms, see the article by P. Korzec, "Das Abkommen zwischen der Regierung Grabski und der jüdischen Parlaments Vertretung," *Jahrbücher für Geschichte Osteuropas*, 20 (1972): 331–266.

30. The first twelve points of the agreement were published in both Yiddish (*Haynt*, July 5, 1925) and Polish (*Chwila*, July 3, 1925) language newspapers, but the remaining thirty points—never officially recognized by the Polish authorities—weren't published until May 7, 1926 (*Haynt*).

31. E.g., Rothschild, "Ethnic Peripheries Versus Ethnic Cores," 599, and Mendelsohn, "Dilemma of Jewish Politics," 208.

32. For the attitudes of the various minorities to Piłsudski's coup, see the standard work on the subject, J. Rothschild's *Piłsudski's Coup d'Etat* (New York, 1966), and the two works by Polish historian A. Garlicki, *Przewrot majowy* (Warsaw, 1968) and *Od maja do Brześcia* (Warsaw, 1981).

33. For example, in the field of education the state legalized Agudath–run elementary schools (*heder*), making them equivalent to public primary schools (and thus eligible for government funding and recognizing the legitimacy of their diplomas). The government also endorsed the Agudath concept of the *kehilloth* as a purely religious institution, over the Zionist and leftist conceptions of it as a secular political body, and inserted ordinances into *kehilloth* statutes designed to facilitate Agudath control of them; additionally, government control of *kehilloth* budgets was also used to bolster Agudath control. For details, see N. Eck, "The Educational Institutions of Polish Jewry (1921–1934)," *Jewish Social Studies*, 9 (1947), 1: 3–32, and N. Eisenstein, *Jewish Schools in Poland* (New York, 1950) on the schools, and W. Glickson, *A Kehillah in Poland During the Inter-War Years* (Philadelphia, 1969).

34. For a discussion of Jewish activity in parliament during this period, see the excellent but hitherto unpublished work by Joseph Gitman, "The Jews and the Jewish Problem in the Polish Parliament,

but more contemporary account is by L. Halpern, "Polityka żydowska w sejmie i Senacie Rzeczypospolitej Polskiej, 1919–1933," *Sprawy Narodowościowe*, 7 (1933), 1: 29–71.

35. The 1928 elections returned 3 Jews on the BBWR ticket and an additional 13 on opposition lists to the Sejm, and 6 more to the Senate, for a total Jewish representation of 22 seats in parliament—as compared with 46 in the 1922–1928 session. In the 1930 balloting, 3 Jewish deputies and 1 senator were returned on the BBWR list, while the opposition counted only 6—4 Galician Zionists, 2 from the Grünbaum group.

36. Assessing this approach, Rothschild observes: "On the one hand, the regime's technocratic ideologues and policymakers tended to view middlemen as unproductive and unnecessary interlopers. On the other hand, they extracted the bulk of the state's tax revenues precisely from the commercial sector of the economy. As a result, Jews, who were overrepresented in commerce and trade, paid 35 to 40 percent of Poland's taxes, although they formed only 10 percent of its population.""Ethnic Peripheries Versus Ethnic Cores," 602. For an in-depth description of how Jewish small-businessmen were affected, see J. Tomaszewski, "Położenie drobnych kupców żydowskich w Polsce w latach wielkiego kryzysu (1929–1935)," *Biuletyn Żydowskiego Instytutu Historycznego*, 102 (1977): 35–54.

37. R. Rybicki, "Polityka Żydowska," in a leading nationalist newspaper, *Gazeta Warszawska* (July 19, 1931).

38. *MZHRL* 3: 13–23. The party also called for the creation of producer, commercial, and credit cooperatives to aid the farm economy.

39. *Pamiętniki chłopów*, nos. 1–51 (Warsaw, 1935).

40. *Pamiętniki chłopów. Serja druga* (Warsaw, 1936).

41. *Sprawy Narodowościowe*, 8 (1934), 4: 475.

42. This segment of Polish-Jewish relations is discussed in detail in the article by E. Wynot, "'A Necessary Cruelty': The Emergence of Official Anti-Semitism in Poland, 1936–1939," *American Historical Review*, 76 (1971), 4: 1035–1058. Unless noted otherwise, the section of this paper dealing with 1935–1939 is drawn from this article.

43. The anti-Semitic posture of the Roman Catholic church in Poland is a painful but essential theme for Poles to confront. For a background discussion, see E. Wynot, "The Catholic Church and the Polish State, 1935–1939," *Journal of Church and State*, 15 (1973), 2: 223–240. The enthusiasm of the hierarchy's anti-Semitism also alarmed Western observers, including the U.S. ambassador, who reported in October, 1937 that "The Catholic Church in Poland is pronouncedly anti-Jewish in its attitude." Quoted in Z. Szajkowski, "Western Jewish Aid and Intercession for Polish Jewry, 1919–1939," in Fishman, *Studies*, 156. It should be pointed out that the well-known Catholic monthly *Znak* devoted an entire expanded issue to the subject "Katolicyzm-Judaizm: Żydzi w Polsce i w świecie" (no. 339/340, 1983), but unfortunately the author had not been able to consult this prior to writing this paper.

44. For details of the restrictions on Jewish professionals, see the article by Mahler, "Jews in Public Service and the Liberal Professions," *loc. cit.*

45. See J. Orlicki, "Szkic wybranej problematyki do genezy tzw. kwestii żydowskiej oraz koncepcji jej rozwiązania w II Rzeczypospolitej," *Przegląd Zachodniopomorski,* 20 (1976), 3:183–195, and L. Yahil, "Madagascar—Phantom of a Solution for the Jewish Question," in Vago and Mosse, *Jews and Non-Jews,* 315–329.

46. J. Cang, "The Opposition Parties in Poland and their Attitude Towards the Jews and the Jewish Problem," *Jewish Social Studies,* 1 (1939): 244–245.

47. Ibid., 254.

48. J. M. Borski, *Sprawa Żydowska a Socjalizm* (Warsaw, 1937). The pamphlet was published by *Robotnik,* the central press organ of the PPS. For a look at the party during this period, the standard work is by J. Żarnowski, *Polska Partia Socjalistyczna w latach 1935–1939* (Warsaw, 1965), which omits discussion of the party's stance towards the Jews.

49. *MZHRL* 3: 252–253.

50. Resolutions passed by the Chief Bureau of the Union of Rural Youth of the Polish Republic (May 2–3, 1936) in *MZHRL 3:* 277.

51. For the congress resolutions, see *MZHRL* 3: 327–332. The press reaction was in *Zielony Sztandar,* July 11, 1937.

52. On the Bund's self-defense squads, see L. Rowe, "Jewish Self-Defense: A Response to Violence," in Fishman, *Studies,* 105–149.

53. See L. Brenner, *The Iron Wall: Zionist Revisionism from Jabotinsky to Shamir* (London, 1984), especially 72–110. For a sympathetic biography by a close collaborator in the Revisionist movement, see the two-volume work by Joseph Schechtman, *The Vladimir Jabotinsky Story,* vol. 1, *Rebel and Statesman* (New York, 1956) and vol. 2, *Fighter and Prophet* (New York, 1961).

54. "Ethnic Peripheries Versus Ethnic Cores," 605.

55. Mendelsohn, *Jews of East Central Europe,* 84–85.

# 3

FRED HAHN

# The Jews Among the Nations in Bohemia and Moravia

In the course of the period from 1900 to 1938, great historical changes took place in Bohemia, Moravia, and Silesia, the lands of the crown of St. Wenceslas. The position of Prague in 1918 changed from that of the capital of the kingdom of Bohemia, a part of the Austrian empire, to the capital of the new Czechoslovak republic. Slovakia and Subcarpathian Russia, which were for many centuries parts of Hungary, were joined to the new republic. The histories of these two parts of Czechoslovakia are therefore different, and so are the histories of the Jews who inhabited these lands. There were two kinds of Jewries living next to each other in the Czechoslovak republic. They were different in language, culture, occupation, and customs. The former Austrian parts of Czechoslovakia—Bohemia, Moravia, and Silesia—were industrially highly developed, and the Jews there were culturally and economically on the same level as and part of the Central and Western European Jewry. They were culturally, nationally, economically, and linguistically distinct from the Jews of Subcarpathian Russia. This latter autonomous territory was mainly agricultural, and the cultural and economic outlook of the Jews there was typically Eastern European. The position of the Slovak Jews was more or less midway between that of the Bohemian and Subcarpathian Jews.[1]

41

The history of the Jews in the formerly Austrian parts therefore cannot be compared with that of the Jews who had lived in
the previously Hungarian parts. Their cultural and economic
development continued to be different even after 1918, except for
the fact that after 1939 many Slovak and Subcarpathian Jews
shared the fate of their brothers and sisters in other countries
where the German National Socialist regime ruled or dominated.

This chapter will deal only—and it is impossible here to tell
the whole story—with the position of the Jews among the nations
of the historic lands of Bohemia, Moravia, and Silesia. There
the Jews lived among two nations, the Czechs and the Germans,
who more often than not were not on friendly terms. The Jews had
lived there for more than a thousand years, and they had to
survive among the two competing nations. Especially after 1918,
when a Jewish nationality was finally recognized, they had to
make the difficult decision of whether to adopt Czech or German
culture and whether to choose the German or Czech way of life.

It is difficult to understand the narrow-minded nationalism
that poisoned the relationship of Czechs and Germans in the
historic lands and that was partly mirrored in the national
division of the Jews there. As Max Brod wrote in his *Prager Kreis*:
"It is impossible to explain to someone who is not from Prague or
who has not lived there for years, the fine and not so fine
variations . . . in the nationality question, where the language
and text of each store sign and street sign becomes a political
problem." The former Austrian prime minister Taaffe is supposed
to have said: "Um das zu verstehen muss man halt ein gelernter
Deutschböhme sein [In order to understand that, one has to be an
experienced Bohemian-German]."[2]

The question of what language the Jews spoke is for many
people quite confusing, as it is well-known that in Prague there
was a concentration of Jews who contributed greatly to the German
culture. For many centuries, the Jews in Prague spoke Czech, and in
the thirteenth century they considered it their mother tongue.
There was then already a large Jewish community in Prague, and
the writings of that time are quite often mentioned, their writers
being referred to as "our teachers from Bohemia."[3] Only after the
settlement of German colonists and, later, the ascent of the
Habsburgs to the throne of Bohemia in 1526, was some German
used. The Jews' written language, however, was Hebrew, and all
of the famous and important works, including the world history
*Zemach David* of David Gans, were written in it.

As a result of Emperor Joseph II's legislation in the late eighteenth century, German became predominant. In his effort to create a uniform administrative language for his multilingual empire, Joseph decreed that Jews had to keep their business records in German, not in Hebrew as they had done earlier, that the rabbi had to give his sermon in German, and that if someone intended to get married, he had to prove his proficiency in German. The most important provision was that the Jewish schools had to adopt a German curriculum.

German thus moved into Jew Street, and by 1848, the Jews were actually Germanized. Most of them spoke German with each other, and many country Jews often spoke a so-called *Judendeutsch*, a jargon consisting of a mixture of German, Czech, and Hebrew. With education, the jargon gradually disappeared, and pure German or Czech were spoken during the nineteenth century. However, the Jews were considered Germans and a foreign element. Their children did not go to school with the village children, but to the German-Jewish or German school. This was later to change, but many Jewish and non-Jewish writers note that in the 1880s and 1890s, as well as at the beginning of this century, the Jews who were living in a completely Czech environment preferred German literature to Czech, and many a peddler had a small library of German classics at home, which he read on Saturday and Sunday. Ján Herben recalled that shortly after the census of 1890 he asked a Czech Jew in Tábor, where there were no Germans, why so many Jews used the German vernacular. He received the following characteristic answer: "A Jew who speaks only Czech with his customers all year long believes that he is something more when he can read Schiller in German. To know German is something like belonging to the nobility."[4] Likewise Viktor Vohrýzek, one of the leaders of the Czech Jews, noted that one impediment to the Czech Jewish movement was the fact that German culture was deeply ingrained in the Jews. He wrote: "Every Jew is a reader. There is not a single poor Jew who does not read books and newspapers. The Jews also lean toward the German literature because their fellow Jews had a great part in its flowering. Heine, Börne, Auerbach made great propaganda for the German literature." Vohrýzek believed, however, that despite their affiliation with German culture, the Jews would in time become Czechs, so long as relations between Czechs and Jews became friendlier.[5] But attempts at rapprochement were only answered with riots and anti-Semitism.

Many Jews, however, despite Schönerer's anti-Semitic propaganda and despite political changes, continued to consider themselves Germans or at least continued to speak German. As long as Austria existed they were Austrians, grateful and loyal to the Habsburgs, and after 1918, they persisted in their preference for German education. In the northern part of Bohemia, the later so-called Sudetenland, there were still in 1938 many Jews who had not learned to speak Czech. In the mixed language regions and the large cities like Prague, Brno, or Pilsen, many Jews spoke German at home and Czech only at the market, with servants, or with Czech friends. In his conversation with Gustav Janouch, Kafka regretted his inability to speak Czech: "I am badly asthmatic," he said, "since I can speak neither Czech nor Hebrew. I am learning both."[6] This seems to be pure modesty, since in Prague almost everybody was bilingual and had to speak at least some colloquial Czech. Kafka probably meant that he was unable to speak and write the kind of literary Czech his friend Max Brod could. Kafka's father Hermann came from a purely Czech village, where his father had a butcher shop. As a young man, like most of the village Jews, he pushed his loaded cart from village to village in the Czech countryside. Likewise, Kafka's mother had been born and raised in the purely Czech town of Poděbrady.[7] In Prague, however, Hermann Kafka became a German Jew, like so many others who had moved to the capital from the countryside.

By the end of the eighteenth century, Prague had become a German city. The Czech language had fallen into disrepute. The bourgeoisie and the intellectuals avoided speaking their native language, and Czech was considered to be the language of the peasants and uneducated proletariat. The centralizing and, in fact, Germanizing decrees of Joseph II, however, sparked a reaction among a small group of intellectuals and some members of the nobility who feared that the Germanization would result in the extinction of the Czech language. A spiritual and cultural revival began that soon became a national renaissance. The Germanized bourgeoisie and intelligentsia found their way back to their own nationality, and Prague gradually became a Czech city again, its German population relegated to the status of a minority.

This revival coincided approximately with the period when the Jews finally left their ghetto, and with the Jewish enlightenment. Already in 1843, a Czech Jewish movement came into being. It was encouraged by Václav Bohemír Nebeský and his Jewish friend Siegfried Kapper, who believed that a symbiosis between the Czechs and the Jews was possible, and that the Jews should be considered simply to be Czechs of another faith. Soon, however, opposition was expressed to this notion: in particular, the Czech national leader Karel Havlíček Borovský, who was not anti-Semitic, insisted that Jews could never become Czech because they were Semites. Whoever wanted to be a Czech had to stop being a Jew. These arguments, made in 1846, were to reappear again and again in a variety of forms. In 1850, however, Havlíček defended the emancipation of the Jews against the overwhelming majority of the Czech people in an article to his newspaper *Slovan*: "We will soon become convinced that the emancipation of the Jews will not hurt us, but will bring us advantages, as anything that is just does. Say whatever you want, but every repression is unjust."[8] Masaryk, in his book on Havlíček (1896), declared that Havlíček's view in 1846 was wrong.[9] Nonetheless, in 1909 he argued that while the Jews could be Czechs culturally, there would always remain a difference of origin, religion, and tradition.[10]

One of the most important theoreticians of Czech Jewry, Dr. Jindřích Kohn, a friend of Masaryk, insisted that just as there were Czechs of Slav origin, there were also Czechs of Jewish origin; both brought with them a great cultural heritage.[11] The Czech Jews wanted to preserve their Judaism; they desired adaptation but not fusion, and this became the constant topic of their publications. "Do we stop being members of the Czech people if we do not forget our Judaism?" was the perpetual question.[12] Most of these publications were at the same time a defense and an accusation, a defense because before 1918 not too many Jews had joined the ranks of the Czech Jews, and an accusation because it was Czech anti-Semitism that had gravely impeded that process.

Anti-Semitic books and pamphlets of the most vicious kind flooded the market and were eagerly read by all strata of the population. In 1897, Eduard Gregr noted that "all Prague is anti-Semitic today," and Ján Herben added, "The whole Czech people except for a few are anti-Semitic."[13] In 1899, at the time of the ritual murder trial in Polna, the Czech intelligentsia were swept up in a wave of hysteria, and Masaryk was maligned and attacked by the press, students, and his colleagues.

Anti-Semitism and bigotry continued to be widespread in the

historic lands long after and independently of the Hilsner trial. As Ján Herben recalls, even in 1930 twenty-two Christian Socialist deputies, among them a former minister of justice (Dolanský), questioned the minister of education about a leaflet ordered for the schools on the occasion of Masaryk's birthday. The deputies hinted that the Jews did indeed require Christian blood, and that Professor Masaryk had erred in his judgment.[14] The Czech Jews tried everything to endear themselves to the Czechs. They sought, for example, to promote interest in Czech culture, literature, music, arts, and the theater. Nonetheless, these efforts were not greatly appreciated, even though it was pointed out that there would be fewer German Jews if there were more Czech Jews.[15] Only after 1918, when Masaryk became the president of the new republic, did the vicious anti-Semitism subside, even if it did not disappear completely. Under the republic, the number of Czech Jews began to grow, and the number of Jewish children in Czech schools greatly increased, particularly after 1933.

The main antagonist of the Czech Jews was a third group of Jews, the Zionists. Zionism came to the historic lands in 1898. Anti-Semitism, both German and Czech, led many in the historic lands to find their way back to Judaism and led some to espouse Zionism. The Zionist student association Bar Kochba soon became a center of intellectual activity. Martin Buber's first lecture there about the character of the Jewry was a great event, and it began his close relationship with Prague. Many intellectuals joined the movement, among them Max Brod, Hugo Bergmann, and Hans Kohn. Zionism was fought, however, by the German and Czech Jews alike because it weakened their own movements. Masaryk's position toward Zionism was interesting. In his *World Revolution*, he wrote that his fight for Hilsner paid dividends during the war in the United States; all strata of the Jews there, including the Zionists, had supported him. Already, before that, he had declared that he sympathized with Zionism because of the moral regeneration it represented; but he did not believe that a settlement of Palestine would solve the Jewish question. In a message to U.S. Jews, he declared, ". . . I know that the Zionist national Jewish movement is not a movement of political chauvinism but the moral revival of your people." And on 21 June 1919, he responded to a statement by Zionist representatives in the following way: "I do not see why in our state, where so many nations live, the Jewish nation could be an impediment. I can assure you that I will translate my views in the political sphere into practice if I will have the constitutional possibility."[16]

The possibility arose, and a fourth group of Jews became a reality—the national Jews. The recognition of a Jewish nationality was achieved by a complicated constitutional process and, as a consequence, the national Jews in 1919 established the Jewish Party of Czechoslovakia. In contrast to other minorities, they could opt for their nationality without regard for their mother tongue. Caught between feuding nationalities and, often, their anti-Semitism, many Jews, while not agreeing with Zionism, were conscientious Jews and they wanted to belong to their own party. The recognition of Jewish nationality gave them a good way out. The Zionists were national Jews, but the national Jews were not necessarily Zionists, yet both could vote for the Jewish Party.

The Jews in Bohemia, Moravia, and Silesia were therefore split in the 1919–1938 period into four groups: the German Jews, the Czech Jews, the Zionists, and finally the National Jews. At the time of the census of 1910, there were about 135,000 Jews in the historic lands. Of these, about 84,000 were German. By the census of 1930, there were only 117,551 Jews in the historic lands; of these 42,669 had opted for Czech nationality, 35,657 for the German one, and 36,778 for the Jewish one. There had thus been quite a considerable shift to the Jewish nationality, especially in Moravia, at the expense of the German and, to a lesser degree, the Czech nationality.[17]

Prague had a Jewish population of 35,425 in 1930. Of these, 6,746 had opted for Jewish nationality, meaning that the remaining 28,678 must have been Czech and German.[18] It is significant, however, that at the election in the Jewish community in 1930 the German Jews received ten seats, the Czech Jews seven, and the Jewish parties seven.[19] It is also interesting that almost half of all the Jews in Bohemia lived in Prague. The city attracted Jews of all strata and nationalities from all regions of the country since it was not only the governmental, but also the economic and cultural center of the country.

For a thousand years, Prague had been a center of Jewish learning, "the mother of Israel." For Jews of all stripes, it continued to be the center of scientific and cultural life. It was a large, fabled city of unique character, full of romantic associations, with intellect running around on the streets. One arrived there to study or settle with great expectations and trepidations, but soon had to accept the realities of life. Before 1918, many Jews, especially those from Moravia, had gravitated toward Vienna, but after 1918, they came to Prague from all parts of the country, and many remained there as physicians, lawyers, or employed in government, banking, and industry.

The question of nationality was for many Jews a difficult one, although anti-Semitism and later national socialism often made the decision often easier. But for all, especially the Zionists and national Jews, the question remained whether to adapt to the Czech culture or to remain within the German culture in which they had been raised or educated. Max Brod faced the dilemma, and in his *Kampf um das Judentum* he considered the problem of not being a German while speaking and writing in German. In Prague, changing from German nationality to the Jewish one meant, by implication, a weakening of the German element there and a strengthening of the Czech. Therefore, Brod reasoned, to do so might be an act of ingratitude to his German education; he concluded that he needed to differentiate between his political and his linguistic needs, explaining, "I do not feel that I belong to the German people, but I am a friend of the Germans, and, besides, I am culturally related to them by language and education. I am a friend of the Czechs, but culturally alien." Brod, who was a Zionist, expressed what many Jews in Prague felt, and explained why so many Jewish writers made a lasting contribution to German culture. He continued, "I will never be able to think, write, or speak otherwise than in German. My linguistic needs also require that...in Prague certain institutions be preserved, associations with German language, German culture, German theater, German newspapers, German schools, etc."[20] Jewish support for German cultural institutions and their use of German as a mother tongue was resented by the Czechs, as well as by the Czech Jews.

The rural Jewry played a great role in the development of the urban one. There was a great difference between the village Jew and the city Jew. The Jews in the nineteenth and twentieth century had a clearly defined class structure and were quite class conscious. They were socially stratified according to their place of residence and their occupation.

Often subject to malicious attacks by anti-Semitic Czech writers, who accused the village Jew of being a money-hungry cheater and exploiter, the village Jews in fact generally enjoyed the respect and friendship of their neighbors. They were hardworking people, peddlers who usually walked with their heavy packs on their backs from village to village. They started their rounds early on a Sunday morning and returned home for the Sabbath on Friday evening. Such a Jew did not have much money, but owned a little house and enough to sell wares to the peasant on credit until after the harvest. Most of the time, the peasants appreciated what the Jew did for them, and a relationship of trust was often the result. Despite the amalgamation of the village Jews with their environment, they did not accept its culture, but remained devoted to Judaism. The joys, the sufferings, and the adventures of the country Jews were lovingly and often humorously depicted by two Jewish writers, Vojtěch Rakous, who wrote in Czech, and Leopold Kompert, who wrote in German. Karel Klostermann, a Czech gentile writer, also described the Jewish country folk with great sympathy and love in his works.

The simple village Jews did not consider themselves poor, and they did not want to be poor; they had their houses and enough to eat. In their villages they were respected, even drinking beer with the priest and the village elite at the same table; but, in the neighboring town, the village Jew had to sit in the last row of the synagogue while the well-to-do, well- dressed town Jews occupied the front rows. Rakous graphically depicts this social inequality in his stories. It was not having less money that wounded the village Jews, but their social insignificance and nonrecognition in the town Jewish community.[21]

When, between 1880 and 1890, most of the peddlers managed to open shops in the small towns and villages, these social differences and the discrimination they entailed were gradually disappearing, but in some places they lingered on. The Jews in these towns now had shops, a few acres of land, and cows and horses. Along with the wares in their shops, many dealt in grain and cattle. Despite the fact that they had to fight off some boycott movements, they blended well into their environment. Their shops and often their homes became social centers for the peasants. The Jews were respected and lived in friendship with their neighbors, the peasant and priest, quite in contrast to the situation in Poland. At the turn of the century, there were no poor country Jews except the traditional migrant *schnorrer* who appeared from time to time in the village or town. By now, the country Jews had fully adapted to their environment, except in the cultural and religious spheres. Despite this adjustment and social, economic, and cultural progress, the country Jews remained faithful to Judaism and its tradition. The synagogue remained the spiritual home; they were observant and pious.

The rural Jews spoke Czech with the peasants and the town people, but sent their children to the German-Jewish school or the German school before 1918. They often spoke German with other Jews, certainly on the Sabbath; and reading of the *Prager Tagblatt* or *Tribuna* was practically obligatory. A lot of these habits changed in the Czech regions after 1918. At least one son usually went to the *gymnasium* and before 1880, often at considerable financial sacrifice, to the university, while the daughters were sent to the *pensionat* in Prague. These young intellectuals from the countryside played a great role in the development of the urban Jewry. They made many cities, especially Prague, a Jewish intellectual center and made important contributions to literature, the arts, and the sciences.

The Jews in Prague, and Bohemia in general, had no real proletariat. The upper class snobs may have considered those who worked for them in the office as such, but the latter really belonged to the lower middle class and not the proletariat. Very few Jews did manual labor, except for some self-employed artisans. The real proletariat was Czech: the Czech was the worker, the domestic servant, the nursemaid, the chauffeur, or the market woman. Nonetheless, the Jewish communities were far from socially homogeneous. There were those families who had a high social position because of their properties and riches—industrialists, wealthy merchants, bankers. Then there were others who derived their prestige from their professions. These two strata of the Jewish population, while not equal on the social ladder, were related. They were called, and considered themselves to be, the "better classes," hardly mixing socially with the next lower stratum of smaller businessmen, bookkeepers, clerks, etc.

While the lower strata of the Jewish society assimilated easily into the Czech environment, the upper-class German Jew lived in a voluntary social ghetto. Common to all, however, regardless of social status, nationality, or place of residence, was a craving for culture.

Concerts, lectures by well-known people, and first nights at the theater were major events; and everyone wanted to attend. Jews from all walks of life, from the city and often from many miles away in the country streamed into the big concert halls and auditoriums or to the theaters to reverently listen to the music or to enjoy an intellectual treat. At these cultural events all classes of Jews were united, whether aristocrat, peddler, or professional. Culture was their tradition, a part of their life whatever their station; it gave them satisfaction and joy, self-confidence and pride.

Just as culture was an integral part of Jewish life in Bohemia, so was religion, as it had been for a thousand years. When the twentieth century approached, with its liberalism, socialism, and nationalism, Bohemian Jews split into several different religious groups. There were intensively religious Jews, mainly in the rural areas. Then there were the Czech Jews. Under the leadership of Dr. Jindřich Kohn, these assimilationists believed in a symbiosis of their Jewish heritage with Czech nationality. But there were also those who were completely irreligious, who often believed in a complete assimilation to the nationality they identified with, considering their Jewish heritage and history to be a secondary concern.

Most of the parents of the famous men born around 1880, such as Kafka and Brod, had come to Prague from the country and made fortunes in various businesses and professions. Most of them remained Jews, but made more concessions to what they called progress, modern times, and cosmopolitanism. Kafka's father went to the synagogue every Friday and Saturday in his top hat and morning coat. But at home, the old traditions were already neglected. Hermann Kafka went to the synagogue not because he wanted to give God his due, but mainly for the sake of his business, his prestige, and, last but not least, for sentimental reasons.[22]

For most of the educated Czech and German Jews, religion had become unimportant. This was the *Zeitgeist*, the spirit of the time. With wealth and education it became fashionable to become a Jew in name only, and some went so far as to cease to be members of the Jewish community altogether. Most of them, of course, were still conscious of who they were; their environment, particularly with its Czech and German anti-Semites, would not let them forget their Jewish heritage entirely. All of them were to have a rude awakening in the years 1938–1939.

The blind writer Oskar Baum, a friend of Kafka, saw the situation well. He observed that their grandparents had been petit bourgeois raised in strict ghetto piety, but that the fathers were, in accordance with political fashion, cosmopolitan, except of course, for their adherence to the state (i.e., Austrian, not German) nationalism promoted by the schools and newspapers.

Constantly working, they strove to achieve social acceptance and recognition and material security.[23] Many of the sons of these upper-class Jews, the German Jewish generation of the 1880s—and Baum was one of them—believed themselves to be at the pinnacle of all progress, intellectually superior, and free of religious "superstition." They did not know anything about Judaism except what they had learned in their skimpy religious education in school. Judaism was an accepted tradition, and they were completely assimilated. At the same time, some of them had begun to distance themselves from the liberalism and views of their fathers. With the appearance of Zionism and socialism, a diversification in the national and religious spheres came to separate the two generations.

Kafka's experience is symptomatic of the changes in the attitude of many young people. In the *gymnasium*, he had read the works of Darwin and the German philosophers and was converted through his reading to pantheism. But his friend and classmate Hugo Bergmann gave him various pro- and anti-Jewish pamphlets to read, among them Masaryk's denunciation of the ritual murder trial in Polna in 1899. This affair and Bergmann's convincing arguments made Kafka conscious of the fact that he was a Jew, and that as such he was despised or merely tolerated as an alien by many.[24]

At the turn of the century before World War I, the Jewish youth of Prague were involved in a wide variety of activities. All were highly intellectual, but divided in their expectations and ambitious in their religious, political, national, and social aspirations. Faced with this situation, the B'nai B'rith lodge "Bohemia" in Prague decided to establish a youth organization, partly as a means of recruiting future members, but also in an effort to mediate between the deeply opposing views of the younger generation by means of a nonpartisan organization devoted solely to the ideals of humanity. The lodge wanted to establish spiritual contact with the young people, bridge the generation gap, and thus assure its own continuity. As the report on the founding of the youth organization stated: "We in Bohemia are in the midst of a violent national struggle which attracts the Jews whether they want to be or not, and which...creates hatred and enmity among them. . . . The younger generation is losing its instinct for solidarity. . . . The knowledge of Jewish history, literature, and religion is decreasing rapidly. . . . The school has lost its essential connection with the parents' home . . . and many of our best, who enthusiastically believe in Judaism, note with horror that their children have no understanding of the wishes and hopes of their parents.[25]

It was objected that Jewish bourgeois society would not support a purely Jewish association, but this argument proved groundless when a group of young people decided to establish the association, choosing the name "Johann Gottfried Herder Vereinigung." Both lodges, the "Bohemia" and the "Praga," decided to throw their support behind the association, both morally and financially; the "Bohemia" also put rooms in its building at the disposal of the association. Established in 1910, the Herder Vereinigung from the very beginning attracted the cream of the Jewish young people of Prague. Some of its first members were destined to become famous figures in German literature. In 1911, the association began publishing the famous *Herderblaetter*, in which Franz Kafka, Max Brod, Willy Haas, Oskar Baum, and many other notable writers made their public debuts.

As was predicted, the Herder association attracted young Jewish people of many persuasions. It itself had no sharply defined political, social, or national affiliation, but strove to be a Jewish association in the spirit of the B'nai B'rith ideal of humanitarian and intellectual activity. Therefore the association supported humanitarian activities, and held frequent lectures by prominent people and, of course, social events. At its meetings, German Jews, Zionists, and even a few Czech Jews and socialists were able to forget political strife and harmoniously discuss such topics of common interests as literature, music, and the arts. An intellectual atmosphere pervaded and provided at least some temporary peace and harmony in the midst of the surrounding strife, as well as a sense of common goals in the face of the gathering storm.

The publication of the Herder association, the *Herderblaetter*, became an important part of the literary and cultural history not only of Jewish Prague, but also of the world. Here the young authors were published who were later known as the "Prague School" or the "Prague Circle" (in contrast to literary "Young Prague" of the turn of the century). Five numbers appeared at irregular intervals between 1910 and 1912. The editor was Willy Haas, who was barely twenty years old. The eldest contributor was Franz Kafka, who was then twenty-eight. Many firsts were printed in the *Herderblaetter*, such as Franz Werfel's

*Der Besuch aus dem Elisium,* and Kafka's and Brod's fragment of a proposed common novel, *Richard and Samuel.* Here, undisturbed by outside interference, the young people could express themselves freely; however, the original hope of the founders that such activity would help to bridge the generation gap was not too successfully realized. As Eduard Goldstuecker remarked in his contribution to the republication of the *Herderblaetter,* the young authors rejected the world of their fathers, and in the national struggles that they witnessed, they could not decide clearly for either of the two parties. Great German chauvinism was alien to them, and while sympathetic to the Czechs, they could not understand their aspirations.[26]

Most of them were free of the ominous and petty national hatred that poisoned relations between the two nations with whom they lived. They had been raised in German culture and had a deep love for it, but they also sympathized with the Czechs. They understood the value and the beauty of the Czech cultural achievement, and they wanted to bring it to the attention of the German public. And here the young writers assembled in the Herder association were the pioneers. Otto Pick, one of the young writers, was responsible for adding a special supplement to the October 1912 issue of the *Herderblaetter* entitled "New Czech Literature." In the introduction, he reasoned, "The German press looks upon Czech literature as nonexistent, partly because of a lack of necessary information and partly for reasons which we recognize, but which are not appropriate for the program of our magazine, which is devoted only to artistic interests. We take note in the supplement of important publications of a literature which appears to be now in a happy upswing."[27]

Otto Pick, Rudolf Fuchs, and Hans Janowitz, who at that time were in their twenties, continued to translate some of the most outstanding works of Czech literature. They disregarded politics and the raging national struggle and emphasized common needs, human goals, and national reconciliation through rapprochement.

While Czech composers had become world famous, Czech literature had remained relatively unknown. Even very valuable works were lost to the international public. The German Jewish writers tried to remedy this unfortunate situation. They became mediators between the two cultures and the world at large. They acted as a bridge between the two nations, introducing Czech literature to the world and world literature to the Czechs through their translations. They were not only interested in

Czech literature, but also in Czech art and music, which they similarly sought to introduce to a broader public. Max Brod's efforts on behalf of Leoš Janáček are well known, and Franz Kafka asked Brod to lend his assistance as well to the Czech sculptor F. Bílek.[28] Brod was also one of the first to recognize the excellence of Jaroslav Hašek's *Good Soldier Švejk* and adapted it successfully for performance in the theater.

In April 1914, Franz Werfel published in the *Prager Tagblatt* a kind of manifesto in the name of the Prague School and of the young Jewish intellectuals of Prague. Issued on the occasion of the first performance of Frank Wedekind's *Lulu* in a small Czech theater, the manifesto rejected the narrow nationalism of the fathers. "In Prague there is a new will and a new intellectual youth," he remarked. "I greet the eagerness with which the German authors have made known Czech poets in German and I also welcome the reverence which the intellectual Czechs demonstrate by performing the German Wedekind."[29] The real pioneer in this area was Max Brod, who, as Kafka said, helped all whenever he had a chance.[30] One Czech cultural figure who was close to Kafka, Felix Weltsch, and Brod, was Jiří Langer, the brother of the well-known Czech writer František Langer. He had spent some time with a Hassidic rabbi in Hungary, and Brod noted that without the help of Jiří Langer he (Brod) could not have written his *Reubeni*. Langer wrote in German, Czech, and Hebrew, and as Brod noted, "he was a real son of Prague and of the three cultures which come together here."[31] While the young German Jewish writers could do more for the Czech ones to make them known to a wider public, both groups communicated with each other, stimulating and helping one another. František Langer recalls that the Czech writers met in the Union coffeehouse, while the German Jewish ones met in the Cafe Arco. He wrote, "The relationship among us was very friendly. We were interested in their work, and we exchanged our first-born works. Brod and Pick already then were taking care of Czech music and literature, and transmitted them across the language borders."[32]

The generation of Jewish writers, composers, and artists that established for itself a place of honor and greatness in the world used the German language, regardless of whether its members considered themselves German or Jewish. They were not, however, a homogeneous group in either outlook or in style. The most famous group among them, of course, was the Prager Kreis (Prague

Circle). The only thing they had in common was the fact that they met in the Cafe Arco in Prague. Usually one includes as members of this inner circle the writers Franz Kafka, Max Brod—who actually was its leading cultural figure—Franz Werfel, Rudolf Fuchs, Oskar Baum, and Egon Erwin Kisch. But among the Jewish writers of three decades of this century one must also number such figures as Hugo Salus, Camil Hoffmann, Paul Kornfeld, Ernst Weiss, Otto Pick, Felix Weltsch, Willy Haas, and Oskar Wiener, who published an anthology entitled *Deutsche Dichter aus Prag* in 1919. Wiener aptly describes describes the relationship of these Jewish writers to the city by comparing it to a passion for a beautiful but moody woman.[33] For some of them, Prague was too insular. They found it to be too narrow a framework within which to live and work; Pavel Eisner characterized this literary environment as a German ghetto in Prague. Some writers left for Germany and Vienna, although they continued to be "sick with an immortal longing for Prague," as Wiener wrote.[34]

Eisner spoke of a threefold ghetto: a German one, a German-Jewish one, and a bourgeois one, in which the German Jewish remained isolated from their Czech environment. It was, he said, a kind of exile inside one's own country, noting that as some German writers became aware of their grotesque situation, they would move to Vienna and other German cities.[35] Franz Werfel, for example, left Prague when he was twenty-two years old. Later, in attempting to describe his reason for going, he wrote, "For non-Czechs it seems, this city has no reality. It is a daydream . . . a paralyzing ghetto. . . ." Franz Kafka reacted with hostility to Werfel's attitude, branding it as a withdrawal from leadership, as treason.[36]

Max Brod likewise emphatically rejected Eisner's ghetto theory as utterly wrong and confused. Such a view, he said, was unworthy of the free and hopeful frame of mind of the Prague Circle; nor did it take into consideration the environment of the beautiful, old city and or the coexistence of its nationalities over many generations.[37] The flight from Prague, he believed, from one's own surroundings and traditions, was too negative an approach, a refusal to search for a realistic solution. Brod was right; there was no isolation, no ghetto, unless one chose to be in one. Since there was no spiritual or other ghetto, the only appropriate course of action was to stay in Prague or in the country, to draw upon one's environment, Czech or otherwise, in an effort to overcome any possible separation.

Brod, indeed, was one of those who found in his environment fertile soil for creative work. He remained in Prague until 1938, when he left for Israel. Likewise Oskar Baum, who had been blinded as a young boy in a fight between Czech and German schoolchildren. (These fights continued to take place far into the 1920s, well after the establishment of the republic.) Before coming to Prague, he had worked as a music teacher in Pilsen. The kind and often smiling man died in 1941, shortly before he was to be deported to the Terezin concentration camp. Kafka once commented that Baum had lost his eyesight as a German, despite the fact that he was never recognized as a German: "Perhaps Oskar is merely a sad symbol of the so- called German Jews in Prague."[38] Max Brod wrote in his *Prager Kreis* that while Baum was no Zionist, he sympathized with Zionist goals. During the Nazi occupation of Prague, he strove without regard for himself to support the Jewish community there, and made superhuman efforts to help those who were in need.[39] Many members of this literary generation, in fact, fell victim to the Nazis, who drove them to their deaths or into exile. Camil Hoffmann died in Auschwitz, Paul Kornfeld in the concentration camp at Łódź, and Ernst Weiss took his life when the Nazis entered Paris.[40] Hans Demetz, the last producer of the German theater in Prague, recalled accompanying Oskar Wiener to the place of assembly for transport to the concentration camp; Wiener told him then, with a sense of premonition, "I loved Germany with all my heart, and I must perish miserably."[41] All of them had been raised on German culture and the German language; they loved them and considered them to be their own.

In contrast to the generation born in between 1880 and 1900 and even before, the generation born between 1900 and 1920 only sporadically produced any German literature of world stature. World War I, the establishment of the republic, the frequent shifting of Jewish children from German to Czech schools (especially in the Czech heartland), the economic crisis of the 1930s, the rise of National Socialism in the neighboring countries and the Bohemian north, and finally the Holocaust are probably all to blame. Two members of this generation who did achieve some international renown were F. C. Weiskopf, born in 1910, and Josef Wechsberg, born in 1907, both of whose works are well known in the United States. Another was Friedrich Thorberg, born in 1908, who wrote his first novel in Prague (*Der Schueler Gerber hat absolviert*), but divided his time before the war between

Prague and Vienna and spent the war years in the United States. He returned in 1957 to Vienna, where he died a few years ago. His novels achieved international acclaim, and one of his last works, *Tante Jolisch*, with its often witty recollections of Prague, was a great success. Another significant writer, who is chiefly known in Central and Eastern Europe, was Louis Fürnberg, born in 1909. He spent the years 1941-1946 in Palestine, and returned in 1946 to Prague. Like Weiskopf, he had joined the Communist party during his youth. From 1949 to 1952, he served as councillor of the Czechoslovak embassy in East Berlin, and at the time of the Slanský trial he decided to settle permanently in the German Democratic Republic: there was no more public in Czechoslovakia for a German-speaking writer, and no publishing house in Prague would have printed his poetry or dramas. He remarked that "the tragedy of my life is that I am a German poet and a Czechoslovak diplomat, a discord defying any solution." Prague was no longer fertile soil for a German writer. Weiskopf, too, left Prague for East Berlin with a heavy heart.[42] The Jews had played an important role in German literature, and in Czech as well. Nonetheless, as Pavel Eisner pointed out in an article on "The Jews and Prague in Literature," the contribution the Czech Jews gave to the literary life of Prague cannot be compared to the richness of the German Jewish writers' contribution.[43]

Czech literature achieved world renown only in the second decade of the twentieth century, despite the fact that the Czechs already had some excellent writers in the nineteenth century, including a small number of Jews and half-Jews (Siegfried Kapper, Julius Zeyer, Frank Gellner, Jaroslav Vrchlický, and Vojtěch Rakous).

The Jews had begun to achieve some greater prominence in Czech literature only at the end of World War I. František Langer (1888–1963), who returned to Prague from World War I with the Czech Legion as a colonel and again after World War II from London as a retired general, became internationally known, primarily for his drama *A Camel Through a Needle's Eye*. Almost forgotten but in the process of slow revival is Richard Weiner, (1884–1937), whose surrealistic verse is often very difficult to understand, but who is recognized as one of the most remarkable writers in Czech literature. One of the most important figures of modern Czech literature was Otakar Fischer (1883-1938). Despite the fact that he was baptized, some inner voice compelled him to think of his past. Among other things, he translated Heine and Kleist into the Czech language. One of Fischer's students was František Gottlieb, best known as an essayist, whose works appeared in the Zionist press and publications. Karel Poláček, who died in the Terezín concentration camp, was one of the most beloved writers of Czech Jewish stories; some of his novels have been made into films. Another Zionist writer, Viktor Fischl, who now lives in Israel under the name of Avigdor Dagan, is still a prolific and well-known writer.

One of the best-known Czech Jewish novelists in the United States is Egon Hostovský. Born in 1908, he started publishing stories at the age of seventeen. A prolific writer in the Czech language, he has produced most of his novels in exile, and they have generally appeared first in English before coming out in Czech.

Most important, perhaps, are those Czech Jewish writers who produced a beautiful and moving literature under the impact of the Nazi occupation, works full of courage and deep feeling and a sense of foreboding about the impending catastrophe. The two most outstanding of these were Jiří Orten and Hanuš Bonn. Orten was born in 1919 and was killed by a military vehicle in Prague. Despite the Nazi occupation, he was still able to publish, thanks to the selfless help of a group of Czech poets and publishers, several volumes of poetry under fictitious names in 1939 and 1940. In 1946, a collection of works written under his real name also appeared. Bonn, who was born in 1913, was killed at Mauthausen in 1941. He began publishing in 1936, producing not only beautiful poetry of his own, but also translations of Kafka and Rilke. His collected works were published in 1947.

Finally, some of the Czech Jewish writers who emerged from the catastrophe of the Holocaust need to be mentioned. Most of their work deals with the fate of the Jews under the Nazi yoke, and much of it is the result of the authors' own experiences. Outstanding among these writers are Jiří Weil (1900-1958), Otto B. Kraus (b. 1933), Ludvík Aškenazy (b. 1921), and last but not least—as a matter of fact, he is one of the best—Arnost Lustig (b. 1916), who now lives and teaches in Washington.

Thus a thousand years of great cultural achievements of the Jews of Bohemia and Moravia found their high point in the last two generations before the Holocaust destroyed them. Paul Leppin, a German gentile writer, testified to the importance of the Jewish writers: "As an Aryan," he said, ". . . I will gladly confess that without the Jews, an intellectual life in German Prague would have existed only as a miserable tiny brook."[44]

The legacy of Bohemia's and Moravia's great Jewish past has shaped the consciousness of its heirs and remained a part of them wherever they are. There was no escaping it. Oscar Baum corroborated it in a verse dedicated to the Jewish writer Richard Beer-Hoffmann:

> Blood of the past to the future one flows
> Blood of our fathers, restless and proud
> Within us all. Who feels alone?
> Thy life is theirs, their life is thine.[45]

## Notes

1. Arthur Ruppin, *Soziologie der Juden*, vol. I (Berlin, Jüdischer Verlag, 1930), 354.

2. Max Brod, *Prager Kreis* (Stuttgart, W. Kohlhammer Verlag, 1966), 69.

3. Dr. M. Güdemann, *Geschichte des Erziehungswesens und der Kultur der Juden in Frankreich und Deutschland* (Wien, Alfred Holder, 1880), 115.

4. Josef Penízek, "Masaryk und die Jüdischen Tschechen," in *Masaryk und das Judentum*, Ernst Rychnovský, ed., (Prag, Marsverlagsgesellschaft, 1931), 129.

5. Dr. Viktor Vohrýzek, *K židovské otázce* (Praha, Nákladem akademického spolku "Kapper," 1922), 43–44.

6. Gustav Janouch, *Conversations with Kafka*, (New York, New Direction Books, 1971), 138.

7. Pavel Eisner, *Franz Kafka and Prague*, (New York, Golden Griffin Books, 1950), 51–52.

8. Karel Tůma, ed., *Vybrané spisy Karla Havlíčka-Borovského*, dil II (Kutná Hora, Knihkupectví K. Solce), 389.

9. Ján Herben, "T. G. Masaryk über Juden und Antisemitismus," in Rychnovský, *Masaryk und das Judentum*, 279.

10. Felix Weltsch, "Masaryk und der Zionizmus," in Rychnovský, *Masaryk und das Judentum*, 73.

11. Friedrich Thieberger, "Spiritual Resources of Czechoslovak Jewry," in *Czechoslovak Jewry: Past and Future* (October–November Bulletin, 1943): 25-26.

12. For example: Dr. Viktor Vohrýzek, *K židovské otázce*; Dr. Stanislav Lederer, *Jsou židé semity a národem* (Praha, Rozvoj); Max Lederer, *Českožidovská otázka* (Praha, Rozvoy).

13. J. Herben, "T. G. Masaryk...," in Rychnovský, *Masaryk und das Judentum*, 289.

14. Ibid., 296.

15. *Kalendář česko-židovský, 1909–1910* (Praha, Spolek českých akademiků), 110.

16. Weltsch, "Masaryk und der Zionismus," in Rychnovský, *Masaryk und das Judentum*, 79, 84.

17. Franz Friedmann, *Einige Zahlen über die tschechoslowakischen Juden* (Prag, Jüd. akad. techn. Verb. Barissia, 1933), 24.

18. *Sčítáni lidu*, dil I (Praha, Stání uřad statistický, 1934), 104.

19. Karl Bosl, ed., *Handbuch der Geschichte der böhmischen Länder*, vol. IV (Stuttgart, Anton Hiersemann, 1970), 39.

20. Max Brod, *Im Kampf um das Judentum* (Wien, R. Löwit Verlag, 1920), 17–20.

21. Vojtěch Rakous, *Die Geschichten von Modche und Resi* (Prag, Tribuna, 1922), 14–15.

22. Gustav Janouch, *Franz Kafka und seine Welt* (Wien, Hans Deutsch Verlag, 1965), 20.

23. Oskar Baum, "Richard Beer-Hofmann," in Gustav Krojanker, ed., *Juden in der deutschen Literatur* (Berlin, Welt Verlag, 1922), 198.

24. Janouch, *Franz Kafka und seine Welt*, 55–56.

25. Report of B'nai B'rith lodge "Bohemia," Prague, 1912.

26. *Herderblätter: Faksimileausgabe* (Hamburg, Freie Akademie der Künste, 1962), xiv.

27. Ibid., no. 4–5 (1912), 47.

28. Janouch, *Franz Kafka und seine Welt*, 154.

29. Kurt Krolop, "Ein Manifest der prager Schule," *Philologia pragensia* (Prag, 1964), 333.

30. Janouch, *Conversations with Kafka*, 138.

31. Max Brod, *Prager Kreis*, 157.

32. František Langer, *Byli a bylo* (Praha, Československý spisovatel, 1963), 158.

33. Rüdiger Engerth, *Im Schatten des Hradschin* (Graz, Stiasny Verlag, 1965), 17.

34. Ibid., 17.

35. Eisner, *Franz Kafka and Prague*, 36–37.

36. *Philologia pragensia*, 335.

37. Max Brod, *Prager Kreis*, 37, 53.

38. Janouch, *Conversations with Kafka*, 114.

39. Max Brod, *Prager Kreis*, 128–129.

40. Engerth, *Im Schatten des Hradschin*, 16.

41. *Weltfreunde. Konferenz uber die prager deutsche Literatur* (Prag, Akademia, 1967), 137.

42. Ibid., 351.

43. *Židovský kalendář 5699 (1938–1939)*, (Praha, Nákladem židovských zpráv), 118.

44. Paul Leppin, "Eine jüdische Kolonie," in *Das judische Prag. Eine Sammelschrift* (Prag, Verlag der "Selbstwehr," 1917), 6.

45. Baum, "Richard Beer-Hofmann," 200.

4

JOHN D. BASIL

# Russian Orthodox Response to the Old Catholics, 1870–1905

Outside a few small scholarly circles, it is not generally known that many Russian clergymen and laymen took a keen interest in the Old Catholic movement as it developed in late nineteenth-century Germany, and that Russian ecclesiastical journals and newspapers between 1870 and 1905 were often filled with controversy over how the Orthodox world ought to react to this Western religious sect. In fact, the ultimate failure of Old Catholicism itself was so complete that few people today recall the name Old Catholic, and still fewer realize that some Russians saw its appearance either as a sign of moral regeneration in the West or as an opportunity to weaken Roman influence among Slavic peoples. Papal infallibility is still remembered, although not universally accepted, but the relations between the small group of German Catholics who gained notoriety by rejecting the decree of papal infallibility and the Russians who encouraged this resistance have been forgotten. This ignorance is regrettable because a study of the Russian response to the Old Catholic movement can tell us a great deal about some inner thoughts of the Russian Orthodox church in the period before the revolution.

An active Russian interest in the Old Catholics came about in 1871, soon after Professor Ignaz Dollinger of Munich began to criticize his bishop for publishing and circulating the decrees of the Vatican Council. The learned Catholic historian and his outspoken followers attracted the attention of Orthodoxy not only by their defiance of Pope Pius IX, but also by their own well-publicized conviction that Orthodoxy still believed the true dogma taught by the ancient Christian church. In fact, the very name "Old Catholic," adopted by these German Catholics to identify their cause, appealed to the East. It was meant to imply that Roman Catholicism after 1870 had become a new religion, one that had broken with tradition and deviated from the true way. The Russians ignored the term "New Protestant," used in Roman Catholic circles to identify Dollinger and his colleagues. In September of 1871, the dissenters held their first important meeting at Munich and both the Russians and Greeks who attended were eager to gain an acquaintance with Dollinger, as well as reach a better understanding of his plans.[1]

By the middle of the 1870s, contacts between the Old Catholics and the Russians had become quite extensive, and close relations between the two or even intercommunion appeared to be within the realm of possibility. The St. Petersburg branch of the Friends of Spiritual Enlightenment was founded by the Russian Orthodox church for the purpose of opening a semiofficial channel for communications with the Old Catholics.[2] It was to publish in Russia and in a Russian translation all the basic documents and correspondence relating to the new movement, as well as to publish in German many texts that the Russians considered essential for an understanding of the Orthodox church. The society was placed under the directorship of its secretary, General Alexander Kireev, aide-de-camp to the Grand Duke Constantine, an enthusiastic promoter of the Old Catholic cause in Russia. In 1872 in Cologne and again in 1874 in Bonn, contingents of Russians, as well as groups of clergy from Greece, Romania, and Serbia attended the Old Catholic congress. In 1875, the Russians played an important part in the so-called Unification Congress among Anglican, Old Catholic, and Orthodox theologians. It was also held in Bonn.[3]

All this action came to nothing. By 1876, hope for union or even continued interest on the part of the Russians was quickly fading. The weakness of Old Catholicism was probably the principle reason. It simply made no sense to waste energy on a small group of religious activists that was not likely to grow beyond the stage of an unpopular sect. Despite the efforts of Chancellor Bismarck to bolster the Old Catholics with state aid, the dissenters attracted only scattered groups of laymen, a handful of priests, and no bishops from the Roman fold.[4] (The hopes of the German imperial government to use the Old Catholics as obedient crown servants against the truculent "ultramontanes" gathering strength behind the leadership of Ludwig Windthorst were not fulfilled.) In addition, the weakness of the Old Catholics may have caused the Russian imperial government to make no effort on their behalf. In 1872, when asked by the German ambassador if he would support the *Kulturkampf* against the Roman Church and by doing so lend moral support to Old Catholicism, Alexander II gave an uncharacteristic reply: "We are at this moment not at all unhappy with the pope."[5] The Russian Orthodox church yielded to its government in all political matters, so clergy support for the German dissenters was not likely to grow to proportions that would be unfriendly to the emperor. In any case, by the end of 1876, the Old Catholic episode appeared to have run its course. No explanation was given as to why interest was lost. The name Old Catholic simply disappeared from the pages of the Russian ecclesiastical press.[6]

Ten years later, in 1889, the Old Catholics made an unsuccessful effort to revive their dying movement. Troubled by the shrinking number of priests serving in the Netherlands diocese of Utrecht, Bishop Johannes Heykamp invited the Old Catholic leaders Hubert Reinkens of Germany and Eduard Herzog of Switzerland to discuss the possibility of sharing resources among the dioceses. The Dutch Old Catholic hierarchy was also invited to participate. A meeting was held and the small assembly affirmed some common beliefs written in a document now known as the Declaration of Utrecht. The practical problems faced by the movement were not solved, but it was agreed to hold an Old Catholic International Congress in Cologne in 1890 and another one in Lucerne in 1892. Subsequent congresses were held in Rotterdam in 1894, Vienna in 1897, and in the Hague in 1907; the last important gathering of Old Catholics, the Eighth International Congress, was held in Vienna in 1909.[7]

The Russians quickly took an interest in the efforts to revive the Old Catholic movement. Scholars and clergymen who had been sympathetic to the Old Catholics in the 1870s attended the international congresses in the 1890s, and they were joined by a new group of colleagues who encouraged close relations or even union with Orthodoxy. A great deal was written on the topic, which now spread beyond the pages of the ecclesiastical press, and much of it was devoted to polemics among Russians and Greeks about how Old Catholicism should be received in the East. The reason for the polemics was the growing strength of a body of opinion that rejected Old Catholicism and advised the Orthodox church against taking an interest in the sect beyond an indifferent curiosity. As Georges Florovsky observed in his brief discussion of the topic: "A vigorous controversy ensued."[8]

One Russian scholar who took a sympathetic interest in the Old Catholic cause was Vladimir Kerenskii, a professor of Western church history at the Kazan' Theological Academy. In his many works, Kerenskii identified the Old Catholics as representatives of an antipapal phenomenon that had been reappearing in European history since its early medieval period. The Old Catholics were a sign or a symbol of a very long struggle carried on against the illegal action perpetrated by the bishop of Rome. If immediate political or social motives contributed to the force of the movement, Kerenskii rejected their influence. His long explanation for the rise of the sect included criticism of Popes Innocent III (1198–1216) and Boniface VIII (1294–1303) while it presented a varied collection of papal enemies such as Arnold of Brescia (d. 1155), Marsiglio of Padua (d. 1342), and Franz Baader (d. 1841) as earlier Old Catholic-like figures. The chief manifestation of these Western troubles had been, of course, the Protestant Reformation. Kerenskii was indeed well aware of the individual human beings who protested against the direction taken by the Vatican in 1870, although the evidence he consulted about the Council was naively drawn only from Old Catholic accounts, but he was primarily interested in using them as historical types, as conscience-stricken sufferers trying once again to restore the West to its original purity.[9]

Kerenskii's work is important because it was typical of the explanations of Old Catholicism to be found among all its Russian supporters. N. Ia. Beliaev, who preceded Kerenskii as professor of Western church history at Kazan', for example, used the same pattern. According to Beliaev, the Old Catholics' rejection of the papal decrees of 1870 and their thirst for the regeneration of ecumenical Christianity was best understood by reviewing Western medieval and modern history. He skillfully used the antipapal polemics of Ignaz Dollinger himself to present his views. His history criticized the Spanish Dominican, Torquemada (d. 1468), the papal positions taken up at the Councils of Lyon (1245 and 1274), Florence (1438), and Constance

(1414–1418), the Roman political claims supposedly based on the Donation of Constantine, and the legal scholarship defending the papal courts in the works of Ivo of Chartres (d. 1115) and Gratian (early 12th century). The Old Catholics were arranged to fit into this big picture.[10]

What was said of Kerenskii and Beliaev can also be said of others. Ioannes Leontovich Ianyshev, for example, wrote far less history than the professors at Kazan, but the rector of the St. Petersburg Theological Academy may have been the most influential Russian supporter of the Old Catholic cause. Ianyshev began his most profound discussion of the Old Catholic movement and the Vatican Council of 1870 with the following significant statement: "One of the prime causes of Church division in the 11th century rested on the ever increasing aggression of the Roman bishop not only over the west but over the whole Christian Church. . . ."[11]

My reading of V. V. Bolotov, A. Katanskii, I. T. Osinin, and many authors who wrote articles in *Tserkovnyi vestnik* indicate that the Old Catholic supporters in the East saw in this insignificant sect of anti-infallibility Catholics an interpretation of Western history that resembled the polemics of the Reformation and some aspects of German Romanticism.

General Kireev, the secretary for the St. Petersburg branch of the Friends of Religious Enlightenment and an aggressive Pan-Slav, followed the same order, but I have separated him from the others because a strong political motive was obvious in both his history writing and his criticism of Russian foreign policy. In a long series of articles and letters written in response to his critics in Russia and abroad, Kireev explained that the evil deeds of Rome rested at the base of Western history and the Old Catholic movement. To illustrate this point, he used incidents of popes embarrassing government authorities rather than theologians. Gregory VII had been wrong to force Emperor Henry IV into a humiliating position at Canossa in 1076 and John XXII had been wrong to excommunicate Louis IV of Bavaria in 1324.[12] The Society of Jesus was significant in Western history only for its political defense of the papacy, and it was Kireev who expressed most clearly the sentiment that the 1870 decree of papal infallibility was essentially a political act aimed at strengthening Pius IX against the authority of Bismarck in Germany and the Italian liberals in Rome. The Catholic church was essentially a political system, and the Old Catholics had resisted this tyranny as had so many figures in past Western history.[13]

Among the Russians favoring close relations between the Old Catholics and the Orthodox Church, it was General Kireev who found what may be called practical reasons to forge a strong bond. Old Catholicism, according to General Kireev, should be supported by the Russian imperial government, because it would be useful as a weapon to weaken the force of the Roman Catholic church in Poland, the western Ukraine, and Bohemia.[14] Inhabitants of these areas were Slavs, the General pointed out, who had been forced or tricked into facing toward the West but who were naturally drawn toward Orthodoxy, a religion that understood the proper relationship between the church and the state. Old Catholicism could serve as a stepping stone or a halfway point for Catholic Slavs on their way to Orthodoxy. It was General Kireev who presented the befuddled Mariavitians to the Old Catholic congress in Vienna in 1909 with the aim of strengthening antipapal Catholicism in Poland.[15] So ambitious was Kireev's plan that he suggested the use of Old Catholicism in the Balkans where the Roman Catholic church, during the pontificate of Leo XIII, was undertaking a propaganda offensive among the local inhabitants.[16]

The other Russian champions of Old Catholicism were not as obvious as Kireev in revealing their political motives, if they had any political motives to reveal. Katanskii did once make reference to "our Slavic brothers" and Kerenskii showed considerable interest in the development of the Old Catholic movement among the Czechs.[17] Moreover, these men knew Kireev quite well, so it may be argued that their failure to renounce his plans constituted collusion of some sort. This evidence all seems somewhat flimsy, however, and does not prove that Pan-Slavism enjoyed a strong base of support in the imperial theological academies.[18] It can be concluded, however, that the Russian sympathizers of the Old Catholic movement depended heavily on a one-sided view of Western history that probably had its origins in the West itself. They also pursued a romantic vision that saw Old Catholicism returning Western Europe to a period of history that had passed away at least 1000 years earlier. They took seriously the Old Catholic claim that life without the pope would bring about harmony, a religious revival, and a religious reunion based on a general commitment to the dogma taught by the ecumenical councils.[19] It is unlikely that such a dream could have remained in focus without the continued belief in the reign of a Satan-like figure who had disturbed European life.[20]

The positive approach toward Old Catholicism encouraged by Ianyshev, Kireev, and Kerenskii did not reflect all Orthodox opinion. A strong and determined group of Russians and some Greeks were hostile to Old Catholicism and warned against taking steps that would tie the Eastern churches to this Western sect. Criticism had been present since 1872, but its voice grew particularly strong in the period between 1896 and 1905.[21] Reservations first began to focus on dogmatic problems, then doubt expanded to include the validity of Old Catholic orders, questions of church discipline, and ultimately to the strength of the Old Catholic commitment to Christian belief.[22]

A great deal of hostile reaction was evident in the debate on the *filioque*. *Filioque* is a Latin work that was added to the most important of Christian creeds by the Roman Catholic church in 1274 to help describe the nature of God in the Trinity. It simply means "and the Son," but its presence changed considerably the trinitarian formula derived at the Ecumenical Council of Constantinople in 381. By supplementing the initial wording, Rome made the Son of God an equal participant with God the Father as the origin of the Holy Spirit. The Holy Spirit, the so-called Third Person of the Trinity, now had two sources, not just one. The majority of the faithful in the Eastern churches opposed both this change and what was later to become known as the *filioque* theology. They insisted that both scripture and church tradition revealed the Father to be the sole origin of the Holy Spirit. Rome protested against the way in which this criticism was made and refused to delete the *filioque* clause. It came into traditional usage in the Western churches. As a counter measure, some Eastern churches introduced into the creed the word "only" (following "Father"), to emphasize their rejection of the *filioque*.

Because the Old Catholics wished to enter a union with the Eastern church, it came forward quite naturally that the *filioque* theology would have to be officially rejected as a condition for close relations. After all, if Dollinger and his colleagues based their faith on the teachings of the undivided church of the early centuries, as they said, why object to discarding what was clearly a corruption introduced by Western medieval churchmen and held steadfastly by the Roman See? The seriousness of the issue was obvious. The two Old Catholic congresses held in 1874 and 1875 devoted a great deal of time to a discussion of the *filioque*, and many well-known European theologians participated either at the congresses or by writing learned analyses that were published in the late 1870s. When the so-called Unity Congress ended in Bonn in 1875, it appeared as though the Old Catholic leadership was prepared to drop the questionable clause from the creed, but the question was not yet settled.[23]

Some Russians remained suspicious. Even in 1875, after the Old Catholic leaders had agreed to delete the *filioque*, there was reason to believe that the official Old Catholic position was not being accepted by all the groups that made up the sect. Moreover, it was suspected in some quarters that the Old Catholic leadership had agreed to delete the clause in its official statements only to attract support from the East. It was a sop given away by men who did not take the dogma seriously and were indifferent to its place in or out of the creed.[24] In 1896, when the subject was again raised, newly formed committees of both the Russian Orthodox church and the Old Catholic International Congress were expected to resolve the issue, but instead of reaching an agreement they entered a controversy proving that the earlier skirmishes had more than simply semantic significance.[25]

Alexander Gusev was an important figure in this controversy. The professor of philosophy at the Kazan Theological Academy and president of the Russian Friends of Leibniz Society presented a series of rather hyperbolic arguments, but in doing so he prodded the Old Catholics into taking a stand that made agreement on the *filioque* issue an unlikely possibility. Gusev pursued the Old Catholics and their Russian sympathizers from 1896 until his death in 1904; at one point, two Jesuits entered the debate, which forced Gusev to fight on two fronts.[26]

His approach to the problem was based on historical and philosophical evidence, but in some important respects his goals were political. As the argument unfolded, everybody agreed with Gusev that the Eastern church fathers would have rejected the *filioque*, had it been presented to them, while it was well argued by the Old Catholics that the Western church fathers, particularly Augustine, would have supported the *filioque*. The debate seemed evenly balanced, but problems were arising because many Eastern Christians were unwilling to accept the *filioque* under any circumstances and because the discussion was drifting into much more dangerous areas. Gusev must have realized what was occurring and saw that troubles lay ahead for his adversaries.

When efforts were made to reconstruct the steps taken at Constantinople in 381 (the place and time of the creed's acceptance), the obstacles became formidable for the friends of union. At this point, the Old Catholics took up a position that was difficult to defend. They held that the authors of the creed stated and indeed fully intended to conclude that the Holy Spirit proceeded from the Father, but, they added, this statement did not say or mean that the Holy Spirit proceeded "only" from the Father. In 381, according to the Old Catholics, the door was left open for those who might later believe that procession came from both the Father and the Son. In other words, the creed did not contain the *filioque*, but its authors did not expressly forbid its later addition. Gusev was quick to point out that the Old Catholic argument was stretched thin at this point, but he scored an even greater victory. The Old Catholics had now done violence to the version of the creed used throughout most of the Christian East, and also had made themselves look like theological speculators.[27]

An unsuccessful effort was made by V. V. Bolotov to avoid the negative consequence of the *filioque* debate. Bolotov was a learned scholar and a devout Orthodox Christian who taught ancient church history at the St. Petersburg Theological Academy. He was a good historian and in sympathy with those who wished to establish close relations between Old Catholicism and the Orthodox world. In his thesis on the *filioque*, which was written in German and first published in the Old Catholic journal *Revue internationale de théologie*, Bolotov introduced a strategy that may have overcome the obstacles confronting the contestants. He advised the use of three categories in which to place all church teaching: *dogma, theologumen,* and *theological opinion.* He then recommended reducing the differences in the *filioque* controversy from the category of dogma where it demanded a strong commitment of faith from Christians to the less imposing category of theologumen. In this category, each side of the argument could marshal whatever evidence it wished, but neither could force the other to accept all its conclusions.[28]

Bolotov's thesis did not resolve the controversy. The Russian and Greek enemies of Old Catholicism rejected it, and even as recently as 1948, an Orthodox theologian reviewing the issue commented that Bolotov lacked a dogmatic sense.[29] Nor did the thesis make a strong impression on the Holy Synod's committee on Old Catholic relations, even though Bolotov himself was one of its advisors.

By 1900, the cause was lost. Those Russians who promoted union, intercommunion, or close relations with Old Catholicism could not overcome the Eastern opposition that depended on dogma as it had been written at the early ecumenical councils and as it was being interpreted in the nineteenth century.[30] They had been attracted to Old Catholicism largely by their animosity toward the papacy and by a vision of renewed Christianity based on circumstances long since passed into history. Some of these motives were shared by other Russians and Greeks, but for Alexander Gusev, Zikos Rossis, and Alexis Mal'tsev, union with Orthodoxy meant conversion to Orthodoxy. No compromise was possible.

### Notes

1. Dollinger discussed his views with visitors from the East even before the Munich meeting. Wilhelm Kahle, *Westliche Orthodoxie: Leben und Ziele Julian Joseph Overbecks* (Leiden, E. J. Brill, 1968), 129. He also tried to attract Orthodox attention by sending an open letter to Russia that was published in early 1871 in *Pravoslavnoe obozrenie*. A most striking example of his interest in Orthodoxy can be found in his lectures: the Eastern church "has clung tenaciously to all that had been established at the time of the great movements and definitions of the fourth and fifth centuries." I. Döllinger, *Ueber die Wiedervereinigung der christlichen Kirchen* (Nördlingen, C. H. Beck, 1888), 38–39.

The Munich Congress was attended by I. T. Osinin, a professor from the St. Petersburg Theological Academy, and A. Dimitrapulos, the learned Greek theologian resident in Leipzig. Both men expressed interest and sympathetic feelings to the newly formed group. I. Osinin, "Staro-katolicheskoe dvizhenie i miunkhenskii tserkovnyi kongress," *Khristianskoe chtenie*, no. 11 (November 1871), 777.

2. *Izvlechenie iz vsepoddanneishago otcheta ober-prokurora sviateishago sinoda Grafa D. Tolstago po vedomostiu pravoslavnago ispovedaniia za 1872* (St. Petersburg, 1873), 231.

3. In 1873, a committee composed of three professors from the University at Bonn was set up by the Old Catholics to work with the St. Petersburg branch of the Friends of Spiritual Enlightenment. Theodorus, *The New Reformation: A Narrative of the Old Catholic Movement from 1870 to the Present Time* (London, 1875), 205, and "Otsutstvie u starokatolikov opredelitel'nago ispovedaniia very," *Tserkovnyi vestnik*, no. 10 (March 1875): 7–10.

The official reports of the Bonn Conferences were written by Heinrich Reusch, a professor of theology at the Bonn University. They were written in a dry and impersonal manner and reveal little about the personalities who attended or spoke at the sessions. *Report of the Proceedings at the Reunion Conference Held at Bonn on September 14, 15, and 16, 1874*, translated from the German of Professor Reusch with a preface by H. P. Liddon (London: Rivington, 1875), *Report of the Union Conferences held from August 10–16, 1875, at Bonn, under the Presidence of Dr. von Döllinger*, ed. Dr. Fr. Heinrich Reusch, trans. Samuel Buel, with a preface by Robert J. Nevin (New York: T. Whittaker, 1876). A Russian perspective on the Bonn Conference of 1875 was published during the month of August in *Tserkovnyi vestnik*.

4. It was well known in Europe at the time that the German imperial government was giving aid to the Old Catholics. "Old Catholics," *The Times*, August 14, 1875, 10. Lillian Parker Wallace, *The Papacy and European Diplomacy 1869–1878* (Chapel Hill: N. C., 1948), 216.

5. Juergen Doerr, "Germany, Russia and the Kulturkampf, 1870–1875," Canadian Journal of History, vol. X (April 1975): 57–62, and Francis A. Arlinghaus, "The Kulturkampf and European Diplomacy, 1871–1875," *Catholic Historical Review*, vol. XXVIII, no. 3 (October 1942): 349, 355, 362. The Russian ambassador to Berlin at this time was Pavel Ubri, a Roman Catholic. This unusual warming of relations between St. Petersburg and the Vatican can be easily explained from the perspective of Pius IX who wanted to prevent Bismarck from enlisting international aid in his attack against the Roman church in Germany. According to Eduard Winter, however, it was the Russian imperial government's fear of the sudden appearance of independent Catholic and Orthodox churches, a new Hussitism, that inspired Alexander II to seek closer ties with Rome. *Russland und das Pasttum*, 2 vols. (Berlin: Akademie, 1961), II, 346–347.

6. Some Anglican clergy and some Old Catholic leaders blamed Julian Joseph Overbeck, German theologian, former Catholic priest, and by the 1870s, zealous Orthodox believer, for turning the Russians against the Old Catholic movement. According to Dollinger, Overbeck deliberately wrecked good relations between the Old Catholics and the Russians because a union of the two parties would have displaced Overbeck's plan to establish a Western Orthodox church. *Deutscher Merkur*, no. 50, September 12, 1876, 429–430. Among the Anglicans, it was Frederick Meyrick who saw Overbeck as a stumbling block to union, especially in his June 16, 1876 speech to the Anglo-Continental Society. On the other hand, the Russians scoffed at suggestions that they were swayed by the intrigues of Overbeck, "Po povodu otmeny bonskoi konferentsii v nastoiashchem godu," *Tserkovnyi vestnik*, no. 26 (June 1876): 3–5. In fact, they had grown cool toward Overbeck by 1875 (perhaps even earlier, depending on how you interpret the Grand Duke Constantine's meeting with Overbeck in Paris in 1874). It should also be noted that some of Overbeck's reservations about the Old Catholics (on dogmatic grounds) had been raised by some Russians as early as 1872,

"Inostrannoe obozrenie," *Khristianskoe chtenie*, no. 9 (September 1872): 172, when Overbeck was still an enthusiastic supporter of the Old Catholic cause in Russia. Kahle, *Overbeck*, 132.

7. This second phase of Old Catholic activity was further removed from Rome than the first phase had been. In 1890, Dollinger died and with him went the restrictions against a married clergy and lay control of ecclesiastical affairs. The decrees of the Council of Trent were rejected in the Declaration of Utrecht (the German Old Catholics had cut this tie with Rome at their Heidelberg meeting in 1888) and alterations were made in the Roman liturgical service. Although it was not noticeable at Utrecht, an internal shift was also taking place among Old Catholics that would soon bring many of them into sympathy with so-called liberal scholarship on questions of church history and then to a relativist stand on questions of dogma. The Old Catholic activity in the 1890s was also international in scope. The Swiss and Austrian influence was pronounced, and in the early twentieth century the Polish Mariavitians accepted an invitation to join the sect. In the earlier period, the chief Old Catholic newspaper was *Deutscher Merkur* with its focus on Catholic activity in the Rhineland and Munich, but after 1893 the official Old Catholic publication was the multilingual *Revue internationale de théologie*. It was edited by the French former Catholic priest, E. Michaud. The appearance of the Dutch Old Catholics introduced yet another dimension. The Dutch Little Catholic Church did not break away from Rome as a result of conclusions reached by the Vatican Council in 1870, but had been in schism against Rome since the eighteenth century. Its presence at the international congresses now tied the anti-infallibility Catholics in Germany and Switzerland to theological positions that had been taken up by the Dutch 150 years earlier. All these new developments made Old Catholicism a far more complicated and divided phenomenon than it had been when Ignaz Dollinger and his colleagues founded the sect in 1871.

8. Georges Florovsky, *Christianity and Culture*, vol. II, *Collected Works of Georges Florovsky* (Belmont, Mass.: Nordland, 1974), 221.

9. Vladimir Kerenskii, *Starokatolitsizm: Ego istoriia i vnutrennee razvitie* (Kazan', 1894), 3–8, 36, 136–137.

10. N. Ia. Beliaev, *Proiskhozhdenie starokatolichestva* (Moscow, 1892), 17–20, 24–25.

11. I. L. Ianyshev, *Ueber das Verhältniss der Altkatholiken zur Orthodoxie* (Wiesbaden: Bechtold, 1891), 5.

12. A. A. Kireev, *Sochineniia*, 2 vols. (St. Petersburg, 1912), II, 97.

13. *Soch.*, I, 7, 118.

14. *Soch.*, I, 336–342, II, 117.

15. *Soch.*, I, 60–61.

16. *Soch.*, I, 27, 29, 83.

17. A. Katanskii, "Starokatolicheskii vopros dlia pravoslavnago vostoka," *Tserkovnyi vestnik*, no. 46 (November 1892): 723.

18. It should be pointed out, however, that the idea of encouraging the growth of independent Slavic Catholic churches was not new to the Russian clergy. Winter, *Russland*, vol. II, 343–345.

19. A typical expression of this view can be found in *Tserkovnyi vestnik*, "K voprosu o starokatolitsizme," no. 24 (June 1896): 772–773.

20. Küppers's conclusions that Russian sympathy for Old Catholicism represented an "ecumenical outlooking spirit" seems in need of some qualification. Werner Küppers, "Die russische orthodoxe Kirche und die Kirchen des Westens," in *Die russische orthodoxe Kirche in Lehre und Leben*, ed. Robert Stupperich, (Witten: Luther, 1967), 246.

21. It is not true that the criticism of Old Catholicism began in Athens and then spread to Russia. Rejection of Dollinger and doubts about the movement had appeared in the Russian press in the 1870s long before it became an issue in Greece. "Otsutstvie u starokatolikov opredelitel'nago ispovedaniia very," *Tserkovnyi vestnik*, no. 10 (March 1875): 7–10, and "Prichiny malouspeshnosti starokatolicheskago dvizheniia v Germanii," *Tserkovnyi vestnik*, no. 30 (August 1875): 2–4.

22. Alexis Mal'tsev, "Altkatholicismus und Orthodoxie," *Germania*, no. 180 and 182 (August 10 and 12, 1898).

23. Three of the strongest contributions to the *filioque* literature in the 1870s were: E. B. Pusey, *On the Clause 'And the Son' in Regard to the Eastern Church and the Bonn Conference: A Letter to the Rev. H. P. Liddon* (New York: Pott and Young, 1876), Joseph Langen, *Die trinitarische Lehrdifferenz zwischen der abendländischen und der morgenländischen Kirche* (Bonn: E. Weber, 1876), and H. B. Swete, *On the History of the Doctrine of the Procession of the Holy Spirit: From the Apostolic Age to the Death of Charlemagne* (Cambridge: George Bell, 1876).

24. Dollinger made regular references to this addition to the creed by the East. "Reden Döllingers auf der II Unions-Conferenz," *Deutscher Merkur*, vol. VI, no. 34 (August 21, 1875): 295. He was inclined to dismiss the importance of the question and was heard to refer to it as logomachy.

25. The Russian literature on the *filioque* controversy that appeared during the episode with the Old Catholics is considerable. Some of it is summarized by A. Brilliantov, "Trudy prof. V. V. Bolotova po voprosu o Filioque polemika ob ego 'Tezisakh o Filioque' v russkoi literature," *Khristianskoe chtenie*, no. 4 (April 1913): 431–457.

26. A. Gusev, "Iezuitskie apologii filiokvisticheskago ucheniia," *Vera i tserkov'*, no. 4 and no. 5 (April and May 1900): 522–553 and 659–679.

27. Vl. Kerenskii, *Chto razdelialo i razdeliaet vostochno-pravoslavnuiu i zapadnuiu staro-katolicheskuiu tserkvi?* (Kharkov, 1910), 39–41; A. P. Mal'tsev, "Starokatolitsizm i pravoslavie," *Vera i tserkov'*, no. IV, 5 (1902): 704; Gusev, *Vera i tserkov'*, (April 1900): 527; A. Gusev, *Starokatolicheskii otvet na nashi tezisy po voprosu o Filioque i presushchestvlenii: Polemiko-apolegeticheskii etiud* (Kazan', 1903).

28. "Thesen über das 'Filioque': Von einem russichen Theologen," *Revue internationale de théologie*, vol. VI (October–December 1898): 681–712.

29. Vladimir Lossky, "The Procession of the Holy Spirit in the Orthodox Triadology," *The Eastern Churches Quarterly* (supplementary issue: *Concerning the Holy Spirit*), vol. VII (1948): 33.

30. The role of dogma as a factor separating the Eastern and Western Christian churches was discussed by Reinhard Slenczka, *Ostkirche und Ökumene: Die Einheit der Kirchen als dogmatisches Problem in der neueren ostkirchlichen Theologie* (Göttingen: Vandenhoeck and Ruprecht, 1962), 191.

# 5

JURE KRIŠTO

# Catholicism Among Croats and Its Critique by Marxists

Lately, we have become painfully aware that the dialogue between Marxism and Christianity is not as easy as was assumed twenty years ago. A contributing factor to this new awareness was the realization that this dialogue must deal with facts and realities that originally were not in the picture. For one thing, people became aware that if the dialogue was to have any bearing on life experience, it must be conducted between communist regimes and ecclesiastical hierarchical structures more than between their academic counterparts.[1] The matter is even more complicated in multinational and multiconfessional settings such as Croatia and Yugoslavia.

In any event, it is important to listen carefully to what the dialogue partners have to say about their own and each other's positions. In this article, I will focus on how the League of Communists of Croatia sees the hierarchy of the Catholic church among Croats (katolička crkva u Hrvata), and on the church's role in the present state of Croatian history.[2] I will also evaluate these views by presenting the church's reading of its role in Croatian history and, for that matter, in the history of any nation. In the first part of this chapter, I will present a critique of religion, and Catholicism in particular, by sociologists in Croatia. In the second part, I will analyze the communist politicians' critique of Catholicism among Croats. I will conclude my essay by a critical evaluation of the communist critique of the church.

Two observations are in order here. First, surprisingly enough, the Communist party in Croatia does not have a monolithic view of religion and of the role the Catholic church among Croats has or should have. Indeed, in its own membership, the party distinguishes between "sectarians" (*sektaši*)—that is, those who accept the reality of religion and try to engage religious feelings in the construction of society. In Croatia, and in Yugoslavia in general, the *sektaši* have dictated policy ever since the Communist party took power in Yugoslavia. The official statements always convey that the party has a different, more open, and positive view of religion, but the party has yet to prove that this moderate group is truly in command when it comes to setting concrete policies and practical behavior among the rank and file (*u bazi*).[3]

Second, there are two groups interested in criticizing Croatian Catholicism. One is, expectedly, the high-level politicians and apparatchiks who are, without exception, party members. The other group refers to itself as "sociologists of religion."[4] Although a good number of individuals in the latter group also belong to the League of Communists, and often uncritically espouse traditional Marxist ideas about religion, they are generally more open to the current Western interpretations of religion. They represent a variety of scholarly interests focusing on religion in general and Catholicism in particular, and one cannot find in this conglomeration of views a common denominator.[5] Some of them actually seem ready to abandon Marxist (not necessarily Marx's) views of religion altogether, and attempt a new reading of Marx on religion.[6] The majority of these "sociologists" are associated with the Institute for Social Research of the University of Zagreb in the Area of Religion (*Institut za društvena istraživanja sveučilišta u Zagrebu iz oblasti religije*) whose moving force is its director Štefica Bahtijarević. Unfortunately, the results of their research are published in mimeographed form and in very limited quantities.[7]

These "secular" groups have their counterparts in the religious arena. Sociologists of religion conduct dialogues with theologians and religious sociologists, whereas party ideologues "dialogue" with the Catholic hierarchy. In the latter case, dialogue more often resembles fierce skirmishes rather than serious conversations. This is an indication that the sociologists of religion generally demonstrate more tolerance for religion than the party members in charge of setting policies toward religion do. Likewise, Croatian Catholic theologians express more openness toward some of Marx's ideas than the Catholic hierarchy does. A partial explanation for this mutual openness between sociologists of religion and theologians lies in the fact that neither of these parties is decisive in charting concrete policies regarding religion or the Communist party. It is the party politicians and church hierarchy respectively who are real "dialogists" in Yugoslavia.[8]

## Critique of Croatian Catholicism by Sociologists

A presentation of Catholicism among Croats that drew considerable attention in Croatia was done by two sociologists of religion, both members of the Communist party, Boris Vušković and Srdjan Vrcan.[9] Vušković and Vrcan's book resulted in a roundtable discussion between Marxists and theologians concerning the issues it raised.[10] Since the majority of subsequent works on religion by Croation Marxist sociologists in one way or another made the Vušković-Vrcan book a focal point of their discussion, it is appropriate to pay close attention to it here as well.

Boris Vušković presents an analysis of the Catholic church as a world phenomenon, concentrating on the periods before and after the Second Vatican Council. He sees the Catholic church before the council as characterized by "fervent anticommunism and antisocialism."[11] The opening of the church to the socialist regimes in the post-Cold War era was, according to Vušković, a strategic move. For although the Vatican council opened some new avenues of dialogue and even some new theological developments (the theology of revolution and liberation theology), these did not last long.[12] The reaction by the official teaching body of the Catholic church to these new trends has been increasingly "reactionary." This reaction, Vušković estimates, is typical of the official church, for the church is characterized by traditionalism, hierarchical authoritarianism, gerontism, and a preference for the capitalist economic and political systems.[13] Once again, the Catholic church is crucified between immanence and transcendence, between its feudal structural forms and the modern democratic system, between the status of a class in bourgeois societies and the contemporary movements that negate the bourgeois structuring of society and the church's place in it.[14]

Srdjan Vrcan focuses more specifically on the relationship between Catholicism and the sociopolitical structures in Croatia.[15] He espouses the traditional Marxist standpoint that religion is the expression of the concrete sociopolitical and cultural realities of a given society. What is new in his approach is that he applies this principle to the socialist countries as well.[16]

In his parlance, religion is a "mystifying expression of real problems."[17] He provides a list of these "real problems" that are responsible for the continuation and prospering of religion. Some of them are taken from the familiar Marxist bag, such as labor and inadequate distribution of realized wealth, but Vrcan also provides us with an interesting twist. An area of human affairs, he says, that can find its expression in a "mystified" form lies in politics, particularly as it functions in contemporary socialist societies. The actual political practice in socialist countries is repressive, which creates a considerably greater number of victims than heroes.[18] The result of this repression is increased religiosity in the population.

Another area that can be mystified is culture. In many socialist countries, Vrcan notes, the existing cultural tradition together with its legitimating institutions have been destroyed or disrupted, and new social and political structures have often been imposed forcibly, which has resulted in the people's utter dissatisfaction. These newly created social institutions have generally failed. Their failure is particularly evident in their inability to provide national identity for individuals, groups, and nations.[19] This state of affairs, according to Vrcan, gives rise to social and national discontent, which, if repressed, as is the case in socialist countries, will most likely find expression in a religious form and within the framework of an institutionalized religion. Moreover, institutionalized religion very often becomes an alternative culture in socialist countries.[20] An additional reason for this, according to Vrcan, is that socialist systems are often perceived as hindrances to personal development and fulfillment.

These apparent failures of socialist systems do not prevent Vrcan from suggesting an analysis of religion on a more abstract level. He speaks of the "traditional consciousness" and of religion as an expression of that consciousness. Traditional consciousness,

Vrcan asserts, "elevates the past to be the universal principle."[21] He contrasts it with "revolution and revolutionary consciousness." In reality, he is saying that the espousal of any political, social, economic, or cultural system other than the socialist is part of traditional consciousness. In the case of Croatia and Yugoslavia, "traditional consciousness" is a valuing of systems, parties, and structures that preceded the revolutionary changes during World War II.

In any event, Vrcan applies his notion of traditional consciousness to the case of the Catholic church among Croats. He believes the strength of the Catholic faith in Croatia and Bosnia-Herzegovina lies in the fact that the church functions as a bastion of the "traditional world," a world that a "significant number of the [Croatian] population" prefers.[22] One reason may lie in the fact that the bulk of the Croatian population experienced the social changes after revolution as having been *imposed* upon them.[23]

This analysis of a particular socialist system established under the leadership of the Communist party is as unexpected as it is frank. It is certainly hard to disagree with, as sociological analyses go. What is much more difficult to accept however, is Vrcan's assumption that these or any other sociological factors are sufficient for an explanation of religion in general and of its vigor in socialist countries in particular.[24] His colleague, Esad Ćimić, corrects him by pointing out that there are some ontologically constituent elements in the human being, which are not affected by sociohistorical changes.[25]

In general, Ćimić is philosophically the most sophisticated of the sociologists in Yugoslavia. He acknowledges that religion's sphere encompasses questions about the nature and meaning of human existence.[26] He also recognizes that one of the fundamental human needs is the "need for transcendence," even though he denies that religion has an exclusive right to interpret the "content" of this need.[27]

However, Ćimić is not ready to dismiss Marx's views of history. In fact, he criticizes Vrcan for failing to acknowledge that a particular socialist system cannot be identical with Marx's idea of the socialist society.[28] But Ćimić does not think that Marx's critique of religion affects religion per se or one's religious sentiments. It is much more effective in scrutinizing religion as a sociohistorical phenomenon.

The subsequent discussions of issues raised by the Vušković-

Vrcan book demonstrate basic agreement among Marxist sociologists regarding its fundamental theses, which were highlighted above. Catholic theologians who participated in the "roundtable discussion" expressed some disagreement regarding theoretical and methodological approaches of the Marxist sociologists, but praised the book as honest and open-minded. Drago Šimundža pointed out the need to look at the Catholic church's positions on particular issues from a global perspective of its theological and doctrinal self-understanding.[29] This perspective may prevent interpretation of the church's praxis from an exclusively political point of view. Jakov Jukić concurred with this assessment, adding that another weakness of the Vušković-Vrcan approach is an *a priori* predilection of the left-wing radical movements and contestation groups within the church.[30]

Marxist sociologists who are mindful of the official party line are more negative than their colleagues in evaluating the role of the Catholic church. Ivan Cvitković (of Bosnia-Herzegovina) sees the church "from the perspective of class struggle."[31] He implicitly justifies the regime's harsh dealings with the Catholic church by what he calls "primitive" opposition of the church (in all socialist countries) to the system, that is, opposition "as a form of reactionary bourgeois consciousness."[32] He interprets the church's opposition to atheism as but opposition to the government's daily politics. This alleged refusal to accept the political reality in Yugoslavia is the reason why Cvitković also dismisses the argument that the struggle between the church and party is a struggle between two opposing world-views.

Finally, some Croatian scholars dealing with religion limit their analyses to legal issues set in the constitution and other relevant documents, which govern the relationship between the church and the state. Ivan Lazić may be mentioned as a representative of this approach.[33] After a perspicuous analysis of the factors that constitute the relationship between the church and the state and a presentation of typologies of that relationship, he argues for Yugoslav socialism as its ideal realization. The argument revolves around the principles set in the constitution, with little attention to the practical treatment of religious people by socialist governments.[34] For this reason, he fails to see that in his argumentation the separation of church and state in Yugoslavia and other socialist countries comes very close to the advocacy of *elimination* of the church *from* the state.

## Politicians and Croatian Catholicism

Politicians make similar reproaches to the Catholic church among the Croats, but concentrate on the ones that are of greater concern to them. In discussing politicians' attitudes toward Catholicism in Croatia and Bosnia-Herzegovina, certain points must be borne in mind. First, all politicians are party members. However, this does not guarantee unanimity either in political priorities or stances toward religion. Another important factor of the Croatian reality is that a disproportionately high number of ethnic Serbs make up the party membership of Croatia, and hold high-level political positions. Finally, for obvious reasons, the party policy toward religion is not always either accessible or evident. Pedro Ramet has pointed out how politicians even from differing clans may change their allegiances when it comes to pressuring the Catholic church.[35] Short of party documents, the state policies toward Catholicism must often be pieced together from public speeches and the media, paying attention to the current leading political forces and their exponents in the media. The most reliable sources of the party's policy toward religion are official presentations by high-ranking members of the party's Central Committee to the same body, which become the basis for discussion and, sometimes, a resolution. As such, they may be considered as statements of the party's official line regarding religion.

One such recent evaluation of the Catholic church in Croatia was presented by Branko Puharić, the president of the Committee for Religious Affairs in Croatian government.[36] As my objective is not to provide a "Who's Who" of Croatian politics but an analytical inquiry, I will focus my discussion, as in the case of the sociologists, on one representative view. I chose Puharić's presentation because of its thoroughness and systematic approach. His view of the Catholic church has since been reaffirmed on several occasions by other high-ranking Croatian politicians, which indicates that it is the view of party itself.[37]

As has become customary in similar documents, Puharić points out the similarities between the Yugoslav government and the Vatican on the level of international relations. He contrasts this with the relationship between the Catholic church and the government in Croatia which, in his estimation, is good but in need of improvement. Puharić sees three critical areas where the relationship between the Catholic church and the government in

Croatia must improve. These are: (1) the perception that the church hierarchy is the political representative of the religious citizens and, thus, the political equal of the Communist party; (2) the perception that the Catholic church is the only defender of national interests; and (3) the attempt at political rehabilitation of the late Cardinal Stepinac.

## The Communist Party and the Catholic Hierarchy

The League of Communists of Croatia reproaches the Catholic hierarchy, and implicitly the faithful as well, for never having accepted the sociopolitical system in Yugoslavia. By failing to do so, the Catholic church, in the eyes of the party, is against the fundamental tenet of the party, namely, the "community of...nations and nationalities" in Yugoslavia; the church is perceived to support "state separatism" for Croatia.[38] The party, on the other hand, takes the acceptance of Yugoslav reality by the church to be the *conditio sine qua non* for an improvement in relations between the Catholic church and the communist government, in addition to suggesting that political wisdom dictates this acceptance.[39]

Puharić points out some symbolic manifestations, such as exclusive singing of the Croatian anthem at religious gatherings, avoidance of the name Yugoslavia, and failure to refer to Croatia by its official name, "Socialist Republic of Croatia," which indicate to him that the church hierarchy proposes itself as the political representative of the religious citizens.

One can almost detect a sense of pleading with the church hierarchy to throw its authoritative weight behind party politicians. Puharić wonders why the Catholic hierarchy in Croatia does not apply the church's old tenet that "every civil authority is from God" to the authority in the Socialist Republic of Croatia.[40] He disputes the stance of the Catholic hierarchy that religious people in Croatia are "second-class citizens."[41]

Puharić admits, however, that political interference with free religious practice exists. He attributes it to "inherited relationships," without explaining what they are.[42] He is probably thinking of political bureaucrats in Yugoslavia, all party members, who still operate from a consciousness in which religion is something to be eliminated and religious people are masses that have to be tolerated, at least for the time being. Many moderate party members agree with this assessment, but their convictions have the hardest time in being shared by the rank and file. The reason may be that their words are not matched by concrete actions, which would effectively accept religious people as rightful members of the society. Catholic theologian Špiro Marasović has shown that the Marxist government in Yugoslavia never approaches the issue of religion from the position of the interest of the people, but exclusively from the perspective of *political power*.[43] Puharić's view of the church's place in Croatian society indicates that the situation of religious people in Croatia and elsewhere in Yugoslavia has not changed. He insinuates that the party cannot allow religious people to have important political and economic positions because the hierarchy would work through them on the change of the political system.[44] One hears an eerie echo of the 1960s in the United States when Protestants distrusted John F. Kennedy because of his Catholicism. So, it appears that religious people in Croatia and elsewhere in Yugoslavia will continue to be regarded as second-class citizens. It also appears that the hierarchy of the Catholic church in Yugoslavia will continue speaking about this painful reality as a stumbling block to the improvement of relations between the church and the party.

*Catholicism and Croatian National Culture*

The second reproach the League of Communists of Croatia levels at the Catholic church is the church's alleged identification with the national interests of the Croatian people. I consider this to be the core of the difficulties between the church and the government in Croatia, but not for the reasons usually given.

The party objects to the church's tacit but recognizable pursuit of protecting the national interests of the Croatian people. Recently, this objection to the church has taken the form of accusations that the church limits the Croatian nation to Catholicism.[45] One can appreciate Puharić's concerns with the possibility that feelings of national oppression and inequality could explode into hatred and vengeance.[46] However, Puharić and the party in Croatia do not seem to be ready to face some fundamental problems the party has at hand. Following Vrcan's study, it is easier to spot the central problem of the relationship between the regime and the church among Croats. The problem seems to lie in the party, and it is a problem of perception. Remembering their recent past, the majority of the Croatian people do not perceive the League of Communists of Croatia as protecting Croatian interests. To put it bluntly, the majority of the Croatian people do not seem to trust their politicians' patriotism. I cannot evaluate here whether such a perception is justified. What is relevant for our discussion is that this perception periodically comes out in social protests against misrepresentations of Croatian history, the present economic exploitation (which results in impoverishment and excessive emigration of the Croatian people), the denial of the Croatian language and identity, and so on. Since the party has exclusive power, it is held solely responsible for these failures. The Catholic church, on the other hand, manages to present itself as standing on the other side of the barricades in this struggle. For this reason, the church is also perceived by people as a defender of national interests.

In this regard, the politicians in Croatia should heed the warning of the sociologists that the people distrust the party because it attempted to eradicate Croatian culture by denying any cultural value to accomplishments before the revolutionary changes in Croatia during the World War II. This is how the party created two cultures in the midst of the Croatian people: one that is turned toward the past, which is nurtured by the Catholic church, and the other, which is promoted by the party, trying to create everything anew, and disregarding the past. Not surprisingly, these two "cultures" run parallel to, and are antagonistic toward, each other.[47]

There are indications that, at this stage of development, the hierarchy of the church among Croatians could support the party if the party demonstrated willingness to reintegrate the Croatian culture and value it in its entirety. One may argue that, due to the complexity of the situation in Yugoslavia, the League of Communists of Croatia is not *politically* in a position to do so, but this is a theme for another discussion.

## Political Rehabilitation of the Late Cardinal Stepinac

The case of Alojzije Cardinal Stepinac is well known.[48] A young archbishop of Zagreb during the years of World War II in the Independent State of Croatia, he did not hide his joy at his people having achieved independence and statehood, however truncated these were. Neither did he hide his outrage at the unjust and violent policies instituted by the then regime. When the communists took over four years later, however, they accused Archbishop Stepinac of treason and sentenced him to sixteen years of forced labor. This affair set the tone for the future relationship, or better, the lack of it, between overzealous, uneducated communist radicals and the stubborn hierarchs of the Catholic church among the Croats.[49]

Obviously, even twenty-five years after Stepinac's death, the relationship between the church and state in Croatia cannot improve without resolving the "Stepinac case." Puharić reveals now that the Yugoslav regime was able to establish diplomatic relations with the Vatican in the 1960s because the Vatican agreed to "put the 'Stepinac case' aside."[50] The fresh flowers placed daily on Stepinac's grave, however, are a sign that religious people are not willing to put this "case" aside. As things stand now, neither is the church hierarchy.[51] The hierarchy wants an international commission to reexamine Cardinal Stepinac's position during World War II and the position of the hierarchy in general, which only irritates the government further. The hierarchy also points out that neither Stepinac's speech at the trial nor the summations of his attorneys have ever been published in Yugoslavia.[52]

## Critical Recapitulation

In this final section, I would like to comment on several issues discussed so far.

First, taking into consideration the factions among Croatian communists who are willing to accept the Catholic population at least as a political reality, my analysis has pointed out that the communist politicians in Yugoslavia still espouse an antiquated view of religion.[53] This evaluation of religion is also the fundamental reason for both a negative attitude toward the Catholic faith and a negative appraisal of the Catholic church's role in the history of the Croatian people. This attitude toward Catholicism, in turn, prevents the Communist party, as Vrcan has demonstrated, from asserting itself as a political leadership that is accepted by the people.

The Catholic hierarchy and theologians do not dispute the right of the party to be governed by explicit atheism, but complain that the government institutions, primarily educational ones, must propagate it.[54] The hierarchy constantly draws attention to this fact as its primary disagreement with the government. Ivan Lalić former representative for religious affairs in the Croatian Sabor, concurred with the hierarchy when he blamed Croatian sociologists and politicians for failing to endorse and propagate Vladimir Bakarić's statement that atheism must not be the mark of socialism.[55] On the other hand, the League of Communists is unrealistic to expect the hierarchy of the church to endorse the *political program* of the party. In fact, this move by the church would be dangerous; it would contradict the church's modern consciousness that it cannot have a political mission. Incidentally, this move would represent the alleged practice of the church in bourgeois societies, which is explicitly abhorred by the party.

Second, one may not have many problems with Vrcan's assessment that the hierarchy of the Catholic church among the Croats is fairly conservative. Although the label of conservatism does not have any real bearing on the discussion of the church's role in the world, the conservatism of the Croatian Catholic church is explained by historical conditions. The church came out of the last world war scared and scarred; it had to worry about survival, not about dialogue. The subsequent development of events did not prove to be much more encouraging. The hard-line policies of the League of Communists of Yugoslavia effected the creation of a quasi-opposition among the majority of the Croatian Catholic population. This state of affairs, as one of the roundtable panelists, Jakov Jukić, observed, is a direct result of treating the church exclusively as a political factor.[56] As could be expected, the church has tried to marshal its forces and present a united front. Innovations and theological explorations into new fields have been looked upon with suspicion, primarily because they might be detrimental to the unity and uniformity of the church. The logic is always the same: the more united and uniform the church, the fewer chances the enemy will have of winning.

The fundamental weakness of Vrcan's notion of "traditional consciousness," as applied to religion, is that his contention about religion being against any social, economic, and political changes is quite unsubstantiated.[57] It would be hard to argue that change for its own sake is more valuable than remaining with what has been tested. This point is particularly important for religion; religion does not advocate values on the basis of whether or not they belong to the past or are created in a revolutionary change. Rather, religion views existing values in the light of God's viewing of the human good as exemplified in his messengers.

Third, what can we say about the alleged identification of the Catholic church with Croatian culture and nationalism? First off, because of the bad press that "nationalism" suffers from, a distinction must be made between nationalism and patriotism, as the Croatian Catholic theologian, Tomislav Šagi-Bunić, said some time ago.[58] He also showed how the documents of the Second Vatican Council encouraged a healthy patriotism without chauvinistic exclusivity. Next, it is a historical fact that Catholicism played a decisive role in the formation of some nations, not in the sense that faith was the source of national identity, but that faith gave birth and nurtured the sense of belonging to a particular nation. This is also the case with the Croatian nation.[59] Finally, it must also be said that the primary purpose of Christianity is not the formation of a nation, but that at the same time, it can be experienced only within a particular national culture. The national culture is the "body" of the Christian message. The church is, therefore, by the proclamation of the Gospel, a participant in the creation of culture, and, subsequently, the preserver and defender of cultural values in a nation. The church is obliged to defend cultural values as an expression of human good.

The Croatian Catholic hierarchy seems to guide itself by these principles, and does not hide the fact that it is willing to protect national culture. This in no way implies the identification between (Croatian) nationality and Catholicism, of which the church hierarchy has been accused. This identification would be, of course, absurd, and there is no evidence of the hierarchy propagating such an idea. For Croatian theologians and the church leadership, the decisive question is whether the Catholic church (and every other Christian church) among the Croatians stands for everything that is judged human, that contributes to human freedom, and that promotes the human rights not only of the Croatian people, but of every man and woman on earth. The defense of a national culture from this perspective is not something "traditional" and backward, but an endeavor to preserve and promote what is human and good. There is no reason to think that non-Catholics and atheists are not important formative factors in the national culture in the Croatian context, but it would also be nothing short of tragic if they wanted to eradicate their own heritage because it is permeated with Christian and/or Catholic values.

Croatian politicians' fears that the Catholic church may become a political partner are misplaced. Ivo Banac has demonstrated that the Catholic-sponsored political parties have never had any notable success with the Croats.[60] Christopher Cviic has also reminded us that the Catholic hierarchy does not have a long tradition of supporting Croatian nationalism.[61] The present leadership of the Catholic church in Croatia and Bosnia-Herzegovina gives unceasing assurances to the politicians that the hierarchy does not have any interest in political power. These are sufficient indications that the Catholic church in Yugoslavia is not a political partner. However, the church is a powerful cultural factor among Croats. Several commentators in Croatia have pointed out that the party could easily eliminate the Catholic church from this competition by coming more forcefully to the defense of Croatian cultural and national interests. The role of the church in this area would simply cease, because there would be no need for its interventions.[62]

Fourth, what about the possibility of dialogue? One of the principal problems of the relationship between the church and state in communist countries is an unacknowledged belief of both the church and the party that they are keepers of truth. This arises out of their respective universalizing visions. The real problem arises when, as Nikola Višković observed, militant and dogmatic tendencies predominate.[63] On the communist side, Spomenka Hribar speaks about "red clericalism," thus designating a dogmatic attitude that operates with "the argument of force, instead of the force of the argument."[64] Whereas the church, accepting the notion of sin, can bring itself to admit wrongdoings, the Communist parties have not devised a system by which they can bring themselves to a similar public admittance.

One also gets the impression that the party politicians and the church hierarchs do not come to each other with an open and clearly spelled-out agenda. The party has created several myths, which acquired the status of taboos. There is a set of issues that cannot even be discussed. One of these issues is the national question, that is, the status of the individual nations that make up Yugoslavia. The myth is, as politicians never tire of reminding us, that there is "brotherhood and unity" of all the nations and that the national question has finally been solved in the present Yugoslavia. The church hierarchy does not seem to share this myth with the party. There are indications that the Croatian people do not share it with them either.[65] There are also indications that the relationship between the component nations of Yugoslavia is coming to the forefront of public discussion. This is an important step, because it indicates that the "national question" is *the* central problem of Yugoslavia today.

This may also encourage the hierarchy of the Catholic church to voice more clearly their own agenda and concerns. The responsibility of the League of Communists of Croatia in the area of national interests is undoubtedly irreplaceable. However, the hierarchy of the Catholic church must play their role with greater imagination. They must take into account the complexity of a multinational and multiconfessional state that renders the protection of the religious interests of their members and the national interests of Croatians as a whole more delicate and complicated. The hierarchy may easily be tempted to wait for the party to first meet their demands, because of the often demonstrated fact that the hierarchy has the people behind them. This is a dangerous temptation: it may draw the attention of the church hierarchy away from the fact that the power to make political decisions is and should be in someone else's hands. Admittedly, a wholehearted acceptance of this reality will considerably complicate the role of the hierarchy, for it will require from them greater imagination and evangelical acumen. At least, they may have to side with those that they evaluate as better protecting the interests of the people. The party cannot successfully work for the benefit of the Croatian nation without the Catholic church, and the church must not allow itself to assume a leadership role in that same work.

Finally, a word about the "case of Cardinal Stepinac." I hope that here, too, some imagination will be used. The Catholic church cannot simply brush Stepinac's fate aside; he has become a symbol of the church's own destiny. It is also understandable that the Communists cannot, at this stage, admit any wrongdoing in regard to the Catholic church and Cardinal Stepinać. Nonetheless, a first step has been made even toward that goal. Jakov Blažević, the state prosecutor at the trial against the late Cardinal, acknowledged that Stepinac was put on trial because he did not want to go along with the party plan to drive a wedge between the Vatican and the Catholic church in Croatia.[66]

Ironically, Cardinal Stepinac might be one of the principal mediating factors of national reconciliation among Croats. He gave an example to the church of how to chastise its weak and unfaithful members who wrong others and how to forgive those that wrong the faithful. In this respect, the late cardinal is a shining example for the church. This is the primary reason why the church wishes to have him declared a saint. The Communist party, on the other hand, may recognize in the fate of Cardinal Stepinac the results of its worst sectarian attitudes and accept religious people as co-workers for the national interests of the Croatian people. They will arrive at a genuine reconciliation in the realization that their common interests lie here.

## Notes

1. This has been acknowledged by the Marxist sociologist Ivica Maštruko, "Razmišljanja o teologiji oslobodjenja" (*Reflections on Liberation Theology*), in *Naše teme*, vol. 25, nos. 7–8 (1981): 1103–1104.

2. This expression has been devised by the church to indicate the inclusion of all Croats living in Yugoslavia and even abroad, particularly those living in Bosnia-Herzegovina.

3. For an objective survey of the recent status of the relationship between the Catholic church and the state in Yugoslavia, see Pedro Ramet, "Catholicism and Politics in Socialist Yugoslavia," in *Religion in Communist Lands*, vol. 10, no. 3 (Winter 1982); "Factionalism in Church-State Interaction: The Croatian Catholic Church in the 1980s," in *Slavic Review*, vol. 45, no. 2 (Summer 1985): 298–315.

4. Truly philosophical studies of religion are rare in Yugoslavia. Andrija Krešić's *Filozofija religije* (*Philosophy of Religion*) (Zagreb: Naprijed, 1981) has been criticized for its inadequacy; see Josip Ćurić, "Još jedna marksistička analiza religije" (*Still Another Marxist Analysis of Religion*), in *Crkva u svijetu* (*Church in the World*), vol. 18, no. 2 (1983), 193–204.

5. See the discussion about the youth and religion in *Pitanja*, vol. 16, nos. 3 and 4 (1984): 43–102 as an illustration of this point.

6. See, for example, Duško Belot, "Marksizam i religija" (*Marxism and Religion*), in *Argumenti*, vol. 1, no. 1 (1981): 29–37.

7. The following is the list of publications issued so far: Štefica Bahtijarević, *Rasprostranjenost religioznosti na području zagrebačke regije* (1969); Branko Bošnjak and Štefica Bahtijarević, *Socijalističko drustvo, crkva i religija* (1969); *Porodica, crkva i religija* (1970); Stefica Bahtijarević and Srdjan Vrcan, *Religiozno ponašanje* 2 vols. (1975); Branko Bošnjak, *Razvoj ideje ateizma i humanizma u filozofiji* (1976); Vjekoslav Cvrlje, Nikola Dugandžija and Vitomir Unković, *Ideje drugog vatikanskog koncila* (1976); Ivica Maštruko, *Odnos katoličke crkve prema drugim religijama* (1976); Zlatko Frid, *Kontestacija u katoličkoj crkvi* (1976); Ivan Lazić, *Pravno-politički aspekti odnosa crkve i društva* (1976); Štefica Bahtijarević, *Sekularizacija suvremenog svijeta* (1979); Djuro

Šušnjić, *Religija i znanost* (1979); Nikola Dugandžija, *Religija i ideologija suvremenog svijeta* (1980); *Religija u uvjetima potrošačkog društva* (1980); Jadranko Goja, Ljudevit Plačko, and Djuro Šušnjić, *Neke odrednice religijskog fenomena* (1980).

8. A more complex "factionalization" has been recently presented by Pedro Ramet in "Factionalism. . . ."

9. Boris Vušković and Srdjan Vrcan, *Raspeto katoličanstvo* (*Crucified Catholicism*) (Zagreb: The Central Committee of Communists of Croatia's Center for Ideological-Theoretical Work, 1980).

10. Authorized texts of this discussion appeared in *Naše teme*, 1091–1148.

11. *Raspeto katoličanstvo*, 127.

12. Ibid., 81–97, 108–116.

13. Ibid., 98.

14. Ibid., 57.

15. Elsewhere, he looks at the global structure and functioning of the church. See his "Promjene u katoličkoj crkvi posljednjih godina" (*Recent Changes in the Catholic Church*), in *Argumenti*, vol. 1 (1981): 65–73.

16. Vušković and Vrcan, *Raspeto katoličanstvo*, 146.

17. Ibid., 173–174.

18. Ibid., 175.

19. Ibid., 176–177.

20. Ibid., 180.

21. Ibid., 185.

22. Ibid., 207.

23. Ibid., 209.

24. Cf. my article "Marxist Critique of Religion and Croatian Catholic Culture," in *Journal of Ecumenical Studies*, vol. 22, no. 3 (Summer 1985).

25. *Naše teme*, 1097. Interestingly, Ćimić observes that if Marxists are not able to take this anthropological datum into account in their theories of religion, it is a serious shortcoming of Marxism.

26. Esad Ćimić, "Religija ne iščezava, ona se mijenja," (*Religion Does Not Disappear, It Changes*), in *Pitanja* (*Questions*), nos. 4/5 (1980), 28–39 (29).

27. See Esad Ćimić, "Religija i odgoj" (*Religion and Upbringing*), in *Argumenti*, vol. 1, no. 1 (1981), 38–51 (41).

28. *Naše teme*, 1095–1096.

29. Ibid., 1114.

30. Ibid., 1130.

31. Ivan Cvitković, "Crkva u savremenom jugoslavenskom društvu" (*The Church in Contemporary Yugoslav Society*), in *Naše teme*, vol. 25, nos. 7–8, 1123–1125.

32. Ibid., 1123.

33. "Odnosi izmedju vjerskih zajednica i države" (*The Relationships Between Religious Communities and the State*), in *Argumenti*, vol. 1, no. 1 (1981), 80–103.

34. A standard political method in Yugoslavia is to point out how the constitution guarantees religious and other freedoms and to explain people's experience to the contrary as power abuses by certain elements within the party. Only one theologian adopts this same line of argumentation, the Slovenian Bishop Vekoslav Grmič; see his "Socialism as it Actually Exists in the Light of Christian Theology," in *Churches in Socialist Societies of Eastern Europe*, eds. Norbert Greinacher and Virgil Elizondo, Concilium 154 (New York: Seabury Press, 1982), 64–69.

35. Cf. "Factionalism. . . ."

36. The text of Puharić's exposé has been published by AKSA, a Catholic news agency in Zagreb, no. 28 (739) (July 13, 1984): 3–19.

37. Cf. the discussion by the Central Committee of the League of Communists of Croatia on June 10, 1985. See AKSA, no. 24 (787) (June 6, 1985), 6–8.

38. Ibid., 6.

39. Ibid.

40. Ibid., 10.

41. Ibid., 8.

42. Ibid., 9.

43. Š. Marasović, "Crkva i socijalizam u jednoj nedavno objavljenoj knjizi" (*The Church and Socialism in a Recently Published Book*), in *Crkva u svijetu*, vol. 14, no. 1 (1979): 159–170. The book in question is Todo Kurtović, *Crkva i religija u socijalističkom samoupravnom društvu* (*The Church and Religion in the Socialist Self-governing Society*) (Belgrade: Rad, 1978). See the review of the same book by the archbishop of Split, Frane Franić, in the same issue of *Crkva u svijetu*, 67–80.

44. AKSA, 8.

45. Cf. the interview of Zdenko Svete, the newly elected president of the Croatian parliament's (Sabor) Commission for Religious Affairs and former ambassador to the Vatican, to the weekly *Danas* (October 8, 1985).

46. AKSA, 10.

47. See Vušković and Vrcan, *Raspeto katoličanstvo*, 215–217.

48. Cf. Stella Alexander, *Church and State in Yugoslavia Since 1945* (Cambridge University Press, 1979); Aleksa Benigar, *Alojzije Stepinac*, (Rome: Ziral, 1974); Richard Pattee, *The Case of Cardinal Aloysius Stepinac*, (Milwaukee, 1953).

49. I dealt with this issue in "Relations Between the State and the Roman Catholic Church in Croatia, Yugoslavia in the 1970s and 1980s," in *Occasional Papers on Religion in Eastern Europe*, vol. 2, no. 3 (June 1982).

50. AKSA, 11.

51. Cf. Franjo Cardinal Kuharić's homilies in defense of the late Cardinal Stepinac in Zagreb's cathedral on the anniversary of Stepinac's death in 1981 and 1985.

52. The journal *Argumenti*, vol. 1, no. 1 (1981) missed the opportunity to publish these materials when it decided to publish other relevant

documents for this matter under the heading "Documents Speak . . . "

53. The Croatian Catholic sociologist, Jakov Jukić, suggests that the source of the crudeness in understanding of religion by "official" Marxists in socialist countries is the adoption of a crude nineteenth-century atheism and a naive belief in science. See "Religija i sekularizmi u socijalističkim društvima" (*Religion and Secularisms in Socialist Societies*), in *Crkva u svijetu*, vol. 16, no. 2 (1981): 116–133.

54. Cf. Cardinal Kuharić's report to the Vatican's Secretariat for Non-believers on the dialogue between the church and atheism in Yugoslavia in AKSA no. 31 (794) (August 2, 1985): 2–5.

55. Cf. *Naše teme*, 1142.

56. *Naše teme*, 1131.

57. Again, Vrcan's colleague Esad Ćimić explicitly denies this role of religion; see E. Ćimić, "Religija ne iščezava. . ." in *Pitanja*, 36.

58. Šagi-Bunić wrote about the role of the Catholic church in the Croatian national struggle in the early 1970s. Most of his writing appeared in *Glas koncila*, and later was published in *Katolička Crkva i hrvatski narod* (*The Catholic Church and the Croatian Nation*) (Zagreb, 1983).

59. Cf. Špiro Marasović, "Crkva, nacija i klasa" (*The Church, Nation, and Class*), in *Crkva u svijetu*, vol. 19, no. 2 (1984): 145–159; also Nikola Dugandžija, *Religija i nacija* (Zagreb, 1983).

60. Ivo Banac, *The National Question in Yugoslavia* (Ithaca-London: Cornell University Press, 1984), 349–351.

61. Christopher Cviic, "Religion and Nationalism in Eastern Europe: The Case of Yugoslavia," in *Journal of International Studies*, vol. 14, no. 2 (Summer 1985).

62. See, for example, Esad Ćimić, "Pristup religijskom fenomenu" (*The Approach to Religious Phenomenon*), in *Naše teme*, vol. 25, nos. 7–8 (1981): 1098.

63. Cf. *Naše teme*, 1138.

64. Cf. *Pitanja*, 96–97.

65. Cf. an interview by the Zagreb University professor, Miroslav Jilek, in *Danas* (October 22, 1985).

66. *Polet* (February 15, 1985).

6

BOHDAN R. BOCIURKIW

# The Suppression of the Ukrainian Greek Catholic Church in Postwar Soviet Union and Poland

The outcome of World War II had catastrophic consequences for the western Ukrainian national church in Soviet-annexed Galicia and Transcarpathia—the Greek Catholic (Uniate) Church. Between 1945 and 1949, the Soviet authorities suppressed the church by arresting its entire episcopate and hundreds of the clergy who refused to break the 350-year-old union with Rome and join the state-controlled Russian Orthodox church. In March 1946, the Soviet authorities, with the help of the Moscow partriarchate, staged the so-called Lviv (Lvov) *sobor* at which a group of intimidated Greek Catholic clergy proclaimed their church's "reunion" with the Russian Orthodox church. The banning, if not the elimination, of the Greek Catholic church in Galicia was followed, in 1947, by its "delegalization" in Poland, the forcible "reunion" of Uniate adherents in the Mukachiv diocese in Transcarpathia in 1949 and (a year later) of the Priashiv (Prešov) eparchy in Czechoslovakia.

While focusing on Galicia in its historical territory, which was divided by the 1945 Soviet-Polish border, this chapter will reexamine and compare the methods and rationalizations employed in the suppression of the Ukrainian Greek Catholic church in the Soviet Ukraine and communist Poland, inquire into the motives of the two regimes for their attack on the Uniate

97

church, and briefly analyze their respective treatment of the
Ukrainian Catholics over the forty years that have elapsed since
the end of World War II.

Prior to World War II, the Ukrainian Greek Catholic church
in Poland embraced over 3.5 million believers organized in the
Galician church province, which was divided into three dioceses
and one apostolic administrature. It was headed by the
metropolitan of Lviv and Halych, who presided over six bishops,
and an apostolic administrator, and was served by 2,387 diocesan
and 143 regular priests. The church had 2,387 parishes and
maintained a theological academy and 3 seminaries (totalling
480 students), 31 monasteries and 121 convents with 459 monks and
932 nuns respectively, 4 minor seminaries, and a network of
educational, charitable, and other institutions, as well as lay
organizations, publications, etc.[1] (See Table 6.1.) Dating from the
Union of Brest of 1596, the Greek Catholic church has in modern
times closely identified with the Ukrainian ethnic consciousness
and the national-cultural revival in Galicia, supplying it with
several generations of leaders, institutional protection, and moral
and material support. It had become firmly entrenched as the
most important integrating and nation-building institution of the
Ukrainians in Galicia, with its primate, Metropolitan Andrei
Sheptytskyi (1901–1944) recognized by all but the extreme Left as
the highest moral authority in the land.[2]

The wartime Soviet (1939–1941) and German (1941–1944)
occupation of Galicia weakened the Uniate church's economic and
social base. The church lost most of its material wealth and its
educational, publishing, charitable and other institutions. Apart
from the human losses, it suffered from the occupation authorities, some 300 priests and many thousands of the Ukrainian
Catholic intelligentsia fled to the West from the advancing
Soviet armies.[3] Shortly after the Soviet reoccupation of Galicia,
Metropolitan Sheptytskyi died on November 1, 1944, creating a
vacuum in the supreme ecclesiastical authority that could not yet
then be filled by his chosen successor, Metropolitan Iosyf Slipyi.[4]

The 1945 Soviet-Polish border left Poland with the entire
apostolic administration for Lemkivshchyna and over one-third
of the Peremyshl (Przemyśl) diocese, along with Bishop Iosafat
Kotsylovskyi[5] and his auxiliary, Hryhorii Lakota,[6] and a
combined total of some 200–250 Greek Catholic priests and
perhaps as many as 650,000–700,000 believers.[7]

The Kremlin's long-range objective in suppressing the Uniate church in Galicia appeared to be the removal of the main institutional barrier to Sovietization and Russification. A more immediate goal in this action was to facilitate the struggle against the massive Ukrainian resistance movements (UPA[8] and OUN[9]) which had been significantly undermining Soviet war efforts in the western Ukraine and frustrating the new authorities' attempts to establish their effective control over the more inaccessible areas of Galicia. Another goal was to cut the links between the local church and the Vatican, which was perceived in Moscow as an international ideological center of "anti-Communism and anti-Soviet subversion" inspiring a Western "crusade" against the Soviet Union and its satellite empire. This objective was pursued not only in the western Ukraine, but also against the Roman Catholic church in the Soviet Union, especially in Lithuania.[10]

The Uniate church could not satisfy the Soviet demand to help bring about the surrender of UPA partisans and the "surfacing" of the nationalist underground.[11] This affected both the Soviet decision to destroy the church and the time chosen for its implementation. The timing—after an initial period of the regime's benevolence toward the Uniate church (July 1944 to early 1945)—might have been determined by the decision of the Yalta Conference in February 1945, awarding the western Ukraine to the Soviet Union, by the now certain victory of the Soviet armies over Germany, and by a favorable assessment in the Kremlin of the progress of its campaign against the UPA partisans and the nationalist underground network.

The decision to proceed with the suppression of the Ukrainian Greek Catholic church must have been reached in the Kremlin sometime between December 1944 and March 1945 and the Moscow patriarchate brought into the action only afterwards, most likely in early April 1945, when it was realized that Soviet policy objectives would better be served by the absorption of the Uniates into the "patriotic" and well-policed Russian Orthodox church.[12] The main role in the "conversion" of the Uniate clergy was assigned to the Soviet security organs (NKGB/MGB) assisted by the local administrative and propaganda apparatus. In spring 1945, L. I. Brezhnev was made chief political commissar of the Subcarpathian Military District; it was military tribunals of this district that were to "try" *in camera* the bishops and clergy of the Ukrainian Catholic church who refused to convert to

Table 6.1 Ukrainian Greek-Catholic Church in Galicia[a] in 1938

| | Lviv AEp.[b] | Stanislaviv Ep.[c] | Peremyshl Ep.[d] | Lemkivshchyna Ap. Adm. (1936)[e] | TOTAL |
|---|---|---|---|---|---|
| Residential Bishops | 1 | 1 | 1 | 0 | 3 |
| Auxilliary Bishops | 2 | 1 | 1 | 0 | 4 |
| Apostolic Administrator | 0 | 0 | 0 | 1 | 1 |
| Deaneries | 54 | 30 | 45 | 9 | 138 |
| Parishes | 1,267 | 421 | 577 | 122 | 2,387 |
| Churches ("maternal") | 1,308 | 421 | 640 | 198 | 2,567 |
| Filial Churches | N/A | 392 | 492 | 72 | 956 |
| Chapels | N/A | 73 | 135 | 10 | 218 |
| Diocesan priests | 1,032 | 450 | 740 | 130 | 2,352 |
| Monastic priests | 61 | 31 | 50 | 1 | 143 |
| Theological Academy Students | 280[f] | 0 | 0 | 0 | 480[f] |
| Theological Seminary Students | 87 | 87 | 108[g] | 5 | |
| Theological Students Abroad | N/A | 4 | 11 | 0 | 15 |
| Basilian Seminarians | 0 | 0 | 31 | 0 | 31 |
| Monasteries: | 14 | 8 | 8 | 1 | 31[h] |
| Basilian | 4 | 6 | 8 | 0 | 18 |
| Studite | 6 | 1 | 0 | 1 | 8 |
| Redemptorist | 4 | 1 | 0 | 0 | 5 |
| Brothers | 201 | 30 | 81 | 3 | 315 |
| Scholastics and Philosophers | 0 | 0 | 59 | 0 | 59 |
| Novices | 55 | 0 | 20 | 0 | 75 |

| Convents and Religious Houses | 36 | 40 | 44 | 1 | 121 |
|---|---|---|---|---|---|
| Basilian Sisters | 5 | 2 | 4 | 0 | 11 |
| Sisters Servants | 22 | 30 | 34 | 3 | 89 |
| Studite Sisters | 1 [i] | 0 | 0 | 0 | 1 |
| Holy Family Sisters | 4 | 4 | 0 | 0 | 8 |
| St. Josaphat Sisters | 3 | 2 | 0 | 0 | 5 |
| Sisters of Mercy St. Vincent | 0 | 1 | 0 | 0 | 1 |
| Myhrophore Sisters | 1 | 1 | 0 | 0 | 2 [j] |
| St. Joseph Sisters | 0 | 0 | 16 | 0 | 16 |
| Sisters | 405 | 272 [k] | 252 | 3 | 932 [l] |
| Novices | 19 | 10 | 62 | 0 | 91 |
| Candidates | 29 | 4 | 9 | 0 | 42 |
| Greek-Catholics (1943)('000) [m] | 1,300.0 | 1,000.0 | 1,159.4 | 127.6 | 3,587.0 |

NOTES:   [a] Excluding Volyn, ethnic Poland, Transcarpathia, and No. Bukovyna.
[b] *Shematyzm dukhovenstva Lvivskoi Apkhieparkhii 1938* (Lviv, 1938).
[c] *Shematyzm vseho klyra hreko-katolytskoi Eparkhii Stanislavivskoi na rik bozhyi 1938* (Stanislaviv, 1938).
[d] *Shematyzm hreko-katolytskoho dukhovenstva zluchenykh Eparkhii Peremyskoi, Sambirskoi i Sianitskoi na rik bozhyi 1938-1939* (Peremyshl, 1938).
[e] *Shematyzm hreko-katolytskoho dukhovenstva Apostolskoi Administratsii Lemkovshchyny* (Lviv, 1936).
[f] The Lviv figure includes both academy and seminary students.
[g] Not including first year students (at least 17).
[h] Not including Basilian monastery in Warsaw, and Redemptorist monastery in Kovel (Volyn).
[i] Not including 6 filial religious houses.
[j] A third religious house (in Zazuli) is listed in Sacra Congregazione per le Chiese Orientali, *Oriente Cattolico., Cenni storici e statistiche* (4th ed., Citta del Vaticano, 1974), 681.
[k] The Stanislaviv Shematyzm does not list the number of St. Josaphat's Sisters.
[l] *Oriente Cattolico* lists higher numbers of religious houses and sisters for some female orders.
[m] *Annuario Pontificio per l'anno 1976* (Citta del Vaticano, 1976), 307, 520, 432, 869.

Russian Orthodoxy (along with thousands of Ukrainian "bourgeois nationalists").[13]

After several days of vicious anti-Uniate propaganda in the local press, the NKGB arrested on April 11, 1945 Metropolitan Iosyf Slipyi, together with his auxiliary, Nykyta Budka,[14] and Bishop Nykolai Charnetskyi, apostolic visitor for Volyn.[15] Imprisoned simultaneously were Bishop Hryhorii Khomyshyn of Stanislav[16] and his auxiliary, Ivan Liatyshevskyi,[17] as well as several senior priests in both dioceses.[18] Subsequently in May, some 100 leading clergymen were swept away by another wave of arrests.

Installed after the arrest of the episcopate, the so-called "Action Group for Reunion of the Greek Catholic Church with the Russian Orthodox Church," led by H. Kostelnyk,[19] was arbitrarily assigned by the government the functions of a provisional administration of the Uniate church in Galicia.[20] Its task was to "persuade" the priests to abandon the union with Rome and provide a semblance of a "spontaneous," "voluntary" movement of the clergy for "reunion" with Moscow (no attempts were made to recruit a mass lay following for this cause).[21]

"Recalcitrant" clergy who remained unmoved by the arguments and sanctions of the "Action Group" were "taken over" by the security organs, harassed, arrested and threatened with article 58 ("counterrevolution") of the criminal code, unless the priests "agreed" to sign their adherence to the "Action Group" and its objectives. Such "conversions" were rewarded with instant release and reinstatement in previously held ecclesiastical posts.[22] In this way, by March 1946, slightly over 50 percent of the Galician clergy had been reportedly "won over" for the cause of "reunion," especially after several hundred of their fellow pastors who would not succumb to terror were sentenced *in camera* to lengthy prison camp terms.[23]

It became clear to the Soviet authorities, by early 1946, that neither Metropolitan Slipyi nor any other Ukrainian Catholic bishop could be "broken" to renounce the union and preside over his church's "reunion" with Moscow.[24] Therefore, two leaders of the "Action Group" (Fathers A. Pelvetskyi and M. Melnyk) were hastily ordained in Kiev on February 24–25, 1946, as *Orthodox* bishops, after the "Group's" thirteen core members were "received back" into the Russian Orthodox church. The purpose of this unpublicized ordination was to "meet" the canonic requirement of episcopal participation in church *sobors*.[25] On March 1, the Soviet procuracy published an ominous sounding indictment of the five imprisoned bishops under the "counterrevolutionary crimes" articles of the penal code—obviously timed to spread hopelessness and fear among the "recalcitrant" clergy.[26]

The so-called Reunion *sobor*, which met on March 8–10, 1946, in the cordoned off St. George Cathedral in Lviv in the presence of Soviet movie cameramen and delegates from the Moscow patriarchate, was chaired by Reverend Kostelnyk and the two (still incognito) freshly ordained Orthodox bishops. It was a carefully stage-managed affair, with all 216 "delegates" appointed by the "Group," no agenda, rules, or resolutions of the *sobor* circulated in advance, and the very event withheld from public knowledge until the *sobor* resolved by an open "vote" to dissolve the 350-year-old Union of Brest and join the Russian Orthodox church.[27] Only then was the new rank of Pelvetskyi and Melnyk revealed to the "delegates" along with the news of the "Group's" prior "conversion" to Orthodoxy. By hastily publishing the official *Proceedings* of the Lviv *sobor*, the "Group" leaders intentionally or unintentionally supplied the first-hand evidence of the arbitrary and uncanonical nature of this gathering.[28]

Paradoxically, the "reunion" campaign did not encounter serious challenges from the then beleaguered Ukrainian resistance movement. It was not until after the Lviv *sobor*, in July 1946, that the nationalist underground (at least in certain parts of Galicia) issued its ultimatum to the "reunited" clergy to renounce their apostasy.[29] While some clergymen complied with this demand or tried to explain to the OUN network the involuntary and, therefore, invalid nature of their "conversion," others would not risk Soviet reprisals. The assassination of Father Kostelnyk in September 1948, blamed by the Soviet propaganda on the underground, was evidently engineered by the MGB itself.[30] There is a growing evidence that Kostelnyk (as well as Pelvetskyi and Melnyk) formed the "Action Group" under duress—once he had become convinced that the Kremlin would not tolerate the *Uniate* church under any conditions. He accepted the prospect of formal "reunion" with the Moscow patriarchate as a lesser evil than the complete elimination of the network of the intensely patriotic parish clergy, to assure that their unique social and moral leadership role would be perpetuated in war-devastated Galician society.[31] His "pragmatic" response bitterly divided the clergy and the faithful.

While the Moscow patriarchate now extended its jurisdiction

to the once uniformly Uniate Galicia, it was prudent enough not to hasten with the "orthodoxization" of the local rite and religious customs, nor to proceed with the russification of its new Galician dioceses. In fact, the formally Orthodox church in Galicia has been able not only to retain its distinctly ethnic Ukrainian character, but also—as Khrushchev's anti-religious campaigns decimated the Russian Orthodox church in the central and eastern Ukraine—to contribute significantly to the ukrainization processes within the Ukrainian exarchate.[32]

One reason for this development was the continuing, albeit extralegal, existence of the Ukrainian Catholic church, which had been markedly strengthened by the return, in the years 1955–1956, of two surviving bishops—Nykolai Charnetskyi to Lviv, and Ivan Liatyshevskyi to Stanislav (Ivano-Frankivsk)—as well as of hundreds of priests and monastics from their places of imprisonment and exile.[33] Another, more fundamental reason for both the manifestly Ukrainian character of the Orthodox church in Galicia and for the survival of its illegal counterpart, the Ukrainian Catholic church, as well as for their peculiar overlapping in the consciences of the clergy and faithful, has been the intimate interdependence of intense religious and national consciousness that has long characterized the western Ukraine.

The new Polish authorities, in cooperation with the Soviet Union, sought to "solve" their Ukrainian minority problem—including that of the Greek Catholic church—by encouraging and then forcing Ukrainians to "patriate" to the Soviet Ukraine, in exchange for the more numerous Poles "expatriated" from the East. The widespread refusal of Ukrainians to abandon their ancestral lands and the Polish use of force to drive them across the border provoked armed resistance led by the UPA, which was reinforced by the nationalist units that moved from the Soviet-held territory to Ukrainian-populated southeast Poland.[34] Nevertheless, about 500,000 Ukrainians, most of them Greek Catholics, including a number of priests, were forcibly resettled to the Soviet Union.[35]

Having repeatedly refused to leave his Peremyshl see, Bishop Iosafat Kotsylovskyi was imprisoned by the Polish police in September 1945 and handed over to the Soviet border authorities in mid-January 1946, but the latter released him after eight days.[36] In late May 1946, Kotsylovskyi and his auxiliary, Bishop Hryhorii Lakota, attended the plenary session of

Poland's episcopate at Częstochowa.[37] Yet a month later, on June 25, 1946, Bishop Kotsylovskyi was forcibly removed by the Polish authorities from his residence and taken by the NKGB to Lviv and then Kiev prison, followed on the next day by Bishop Lakota and four senior diocesan priests.[38] The "expatriated" Roman Catholic clergy from the western Ukraine seized the Ukrainian Catholic cathedral, while the authorities confiscated the episcopal residence and other diocesan property, including historical treasures, archives, and the library.[39] Apparently, neither Primate August Hlond nor any other Polish bishop protested against violence done to their fellow bishops.[40]

In the absence of the bishops who were awaiting their "trial" in the Kiev prison, the Holy See named in December 1946 Primate Hlond an Apostolic delegate for the Greek Catholic rite in Poland.[41] On April 1, 1947, he appointed Canon Vasyl Hrynyk, a senior member of the Peremyshl chapter as his vicar general for Ukrainian Catholics, a function that he carried out under extremely difficult circumstances for the next thirty years.[42]

By the end of April 1947, the Warsaw government, in cooperation with the Soviet Union and Czechoslovakia, launched the so-called Operation Vistula aimed at the final suppression of the armed Ukrainian resistance by massive military and police search-and-destroy operations.[43] At the same time, allegedly to deprive the UPA-OUN network of popular support, the government ordered a summary deportation of all Ukrainians from southeast Poland to the "recovered territories" in northern and western Poland. By August 1947, about 160,000 Ukrainians, mostly Greek Catholics, were forcibly transferred to these new territories, where they were dispersed in small groups among Polish villages largely populated by hostile "expatriates" from the Ukraine.[44] Several thousand Ukrainians were shipped to the Jaworzno concentration camp in Silesia, including two dozen Uniate priests.[45] A few more Ukrainian clergymen were imprisoned in other localities.[46] Most of the remaining eighty Greek Catholic priests dispersed across Poland, seeking to continue their priestly functions as biritual or Latin chaplains in convents or as assistant parish priests, at the price of separation from their wives and children. With one exception (Reverend M. Ripetskyi), the Greek Catholic clergy could not openly minister in their rite to Ukrainian Catholics for almost a decade.[47]

Largely isolated from their pastors, the Uniate believers were subjected to conflicting pressures of latinization and polonization fostered by the Roman Catholic church on the one hand, and "conversion" to Orthodoxy on the other, under the Moscow-controlled Polish Orthodox church. Significantly, the latter was headed, from 1951 to 1959, by Metropolitan Makarii Oksiiuk, who earlier presided over the "reunion" of Galician and Transcarpathian Uniates in the years 1945–1949.[48] In the meantime, the property of Greek Catholic priests, most of which has already been seized by the local authorities, was retroactively nationalized by a government decree of September 5, 1947.[49] The seizure of the Ukrainian church's property was legalized retroactively only on September 28, 1949 (by a decree amending the former measure), under the pretext that it belonged to "juridical persons" whose "existence and activities lost their purpose as a result of resettlement of their members to the USSR."[50] This was the only *published* decree that indirectly "delegalized" the Greek Catholic church in Poland; it is still cited in Polish confessional law texts as the basis for the "nonexistence" of this church and "nonrecognition" of the "Greek Catholic rite."[51]

There is no doubt that the suppression of the Greek Catholic church in Poland was a measure coordinated with and demanded by the dominant Soviet power, apart from being motivated by the hostility to Ukrainians shared by the new regime and a significant section of Polish society and the Roman Catholic church. Just as the ultimate deportation of Ukrainian Catholic bishops from Peremyshl followed the so-called Lviv *sobor*, the 1949 decree closely followed the suppression of the last Uniate diocese in the Soviet Union—the Mukachiv-Uzhhorod eparchy.[52] The Warsaw government apparently accepted officially the Soviet claim that the Uniate church had "ceased to exist" in what constituted the Galician sees (although, precisely speaking, neither the Polish part of the Peremyshl diocese nor the apostolic administration for Lemkivshchyna were "represented" at the 1946 *sobor*. However, mindful of the powerful Polish Roman Catholic church, the Polish government did not proceed beyond facilitating "conversion" propaganda among the dispersed Ukrainian Uniates by the Polish Orthodox church, stopping short of staging a formal "reunion" that could have evoked the Polish memories of the tsarist persecution of Uniate Catholics in the Kholm (Chelm) region in the 1870s.

The Polish church, while clearly favoring latinization and polonization of the Ukrainian Uniates,[53] offered an institutional haven to individual Greek Catholic clergymen, but, as a rule, only by having them assume functions of Roman Catholic clergy.[54] With no new candidates for Greek Catholic priesthood admitted to Polish theological schools, this generation of the Uniate clergy might have been expected to be the last.

Reporting in March 1948 to Bishop Ivan Buchko in Rome, Vicar-General Vasyl Hrynyk listed a total of 111 Greek Catholic priests left in Poland (including 53 from the Peremyshl diocese, 37 from the Lemkivshchyna administration, and 14 monastic—all but one Basilians), as well as 4 seminarians, 3 Basilian brothers, and 112 nuns (including 50 Josephite sisters and 49 sister's servants). He estimated the size of the dispersed Ukrainian Catholic flock in Poland at 80,000 to 100,000 and pessimistically prognosticated that "deprived of intelligentsia and the clergy of their own, [they] will very fast submit to this [assimilation] process."[55]

It was only in 1957, after the "Polish October," the rise of Gomuka, and return from confinement of Cardinal Stefan Wyszynski (who, along with the post of primate received that of an apostolic delegate—later *ordinarius*—for the Greek Catholic and Armenian rites), that Ukrainian Greek Catholics—more numerous than estimated by Hrynyk in 1948—were able to receive spiritual care from their own clergy.[56] Under an unpublished church-state *modus vivendi*, the government offered a "tolerated but not recognized" status to the Greek Catholic *rite* within the Polish Roman Catholic church, allowing some fifty surviving Greek Catholic priests to serve as *biritual* assistants in Roman Catholic parishes with a large concentration of Ukrainians and to provide occasional liturgical services in some fifty "pastoral points."[57] No juridical person status or property rights have been restored to the Greek Catholic *church*. Contained by severe administrative restrictions and police surveillance, as much as by surviving ukrainophobia in the lower reaches of the Polish church, the Ukrainian Catholics have not been able to reactivate the Peremyshl diocese and to fill the see vacated by Bishop Kotsylovskyi in 1946.[58] Significantly, the Polish censors have been ordered by the regime to eliminate any information (in the media) about "the existence—actually in Poland—of the Greek Catholic rite, its subordination to [Cardinal] Wyszynski, as well as any activities of the Uniates in our country."[59]

While initially, in the mid-1940s, there seemed to be little difference in Soviet and Polish policies toward the Ukrainian

Catholic church—perceived by both Moscow and Warsaw as the chief spiritual and institutional obstacle to their nationality policies, the Stalinist formula of forcible reunion with the Russian Orthodox church and repudiation of the union with Rome could not be applied under Polish conditions, where the powerful Roman Catholic church grudgingly extended its protective wing over the remnants of the Greek Catholic church. Post-1956 evolution in both Soviet and Polish domestic politics favored the reemergence of the Ukrainian Uniate church. In the western Ukraine, the return from the GULAG of the Uniate clergy (including two bishops) made it possible to rebuild a catacomb church protected from another mass liquidation by the fragile de-Stalinization measures, the relaxation in the Moscow-Vatican relations, and its massive popular support base.[60] In Poland, the dynamics of Warsaw government's religious and minorities policies moved toward greater relaxation of state controls and a diminution of Soviet influence over Polish domestic affairs. The Ukrainian Greek Catholic church—officially "nonexistent" but grudgingly tolerated by the authorities—was one of the beneficiaries of these trends, even if the Soviet veto over formal legalization of this church has remained in effect,[61] bolstered by the widely shared Polish desire never to allow Ukrainians to reclaim their ancestral lands in southwestern Poland (even in such a symbolic fashion as the filling of their vacant Peremyshl episcopal see).[62]

The ascendance in 1978 of former archbishop of Kraków, Karol Cardinal Wojtyła, to the throne of St. Peter and repeated manifestations of his solicitude for the Ukrainian church, have brought a significant improvement in the treatment of the Ukrainian Catholics in Poland.[63] This is reflected in the ordination, by officially visiting Ukrainian bishops, since 1981, of twelve new Ukrainian Catholic priests (over the previous thirty years only ten priests were ordained);[64] a relatively large number of candidates for priesthood;[65] the allocation to Ukrainian Catholic congregations of some twenty churches for continuous use; and declining societal hostility to Ukrainians.[66] In the Ukraine, however, the reversal by John Paul II of his predecessors' *Ostpolitik* has led the regime to intensify its persecution of the illegal Ukrainian Catholic church and evoked new forms of dissidence in defense of this largest banned church in the Soviet empire.[67]

## Notes

1. For detailed 1938 statistical data on the three Galician dioceses, see Table 6.1, which also incorporates the 1936 data on the apostolic administration for Lemkivshchyna, which, by a Polish-Vatican agreement, was separated from the Peremyshl diocese in February 1934.

2. Born on July 26, 1865, in Prylbychi, Galicia, Count Roman Sheptytskyi was allowed to transfer from the Latin to the Eastern rite at the age of 23. Having entered the Basilian Order, he assumed the name of Andrei and was ordained a priest in 1892. Appointed abbot of the Lviv Basilian monastery, Sheptytskyi was consecrated, in 1899, bishop of Stanislaviv (Stanislav), and in December 1900 named by Pope Leo XIII as archbishop of Lviv and Halych, metropolitan of Galicia. In 1908, Sheptytskyi was also unofficially delegated by Pope Pius X special powers for Russia. With the wartime Russian occupation of Galicia (1914–1915), Metropolitan Andrei was exiled in September 1914 to inner Russia. Upon his release by the Provisional Government in 1917, Sheptytskyi convened in Petrograd a synod, at which the Russian Greek Catholic church was formed, under Exarch Leonid Fedorov. The metropolitan's support for the western Ukrainian National Republic (proclaimed in November 1918), which was invaded by a reborn Poland and eventually occupied by the summer of 1919, led to his house arrest and the subsequent three-year stay in the West. Partly paralyzed since the early 1930s, Sheptytskyi continued his manifold activities during the World War II Soviet and German occupations of Galicia. He died, shortly after Soviet reoccupation of Galicia, on November 1, 1944. For the best available biography of Metropolitan Sheptytskyi, see Cyrille Korolevskij, *Metropolite André Szeptyckyj*, 1886–1944 (Rome, 1964).

3. See *Shematyzm dukhovenstva Ukrainskoi Katolytskoi Tserkvy v Nimechchyni* (Munich, 1947).

4. Iosyf Slipyi was born on February 17, 1892, in Zazdrist, Galicia; he was ordained a priest in September 1917; appointed rector of the Lviv theological seminary (1926) and academy (1929), consecrated titular archbishop of Serra and coadjutor by Metropolitan Sheptytskyi in December 1939, and succeeded the latter on November 1, 1944. Arrested by the Soviet police in April 1945 and sentenced in 1946 to eight years, he was subsequently exiled in 1953 to Siberia. Rearrested there again in June 1958, Metropolitan Slipyi was sentenced to another term of seven years. Released by a Supreme Soviet Presidium decree in January 1963, he arrived at the Vatican in February 1963 and was confirmed as archbishop-major of Lviv for Ukrainians. Named cardinal by Pope Paul VI in February 1965, Iosyf Slipyi assumed in 1975 the title of patriarch. He died in Rome on September 7, 1984.

5. Born on March 3, 1896, in Pakoshivka, western Galicia, Kotsylovskyi was ordained as priest in 1907 and entered the Basilian order in 1911; he was nominated bishop of Peremyshl, Sambir, and

Sianik in November 1916, and consecrated in September 1917. He remained in Peremyshl, after the city was ceded to Poland by the Soviet Union in 1944. Arrested by the Polish security police in September 1945 and, again, in June 1946, Bishop Kotsylovskyi was handed over to the Soviet police and died while awaiting trial in the Kiev prison on November 17, 1947.

6. Lakota was born on January 31, 1883. Ordained as priest in 1908, he was appointed rector of the Peremyshl theological seminary in 1918, and was named titular bishop of Daonio and auxiliary to Bishop Kotsylovskyi in 1926. Arrested and handed over to the Soviet police along with Bishop Kotsylovskyi in June 1946, Lakota was sentenced *in camera* in Kiev, and died on November 12, 1950 in the Vorkuta forced labor camp.

7. Calculated on the basis of the 1938 Peremyshl and 1936 Lemkivshchyna *shematyzm*; and a lengthy confidential report to Bishop Ivan Buchko in Rome, "Tserkva v ridnomu kraiu i v Polshchi" (*The Church in the Native Land and in Poland*), dispatched on March 18, 1948 by Canon Vasyl Hrynyk, vicar-general for Greek Catholics in Poland (hereafter the Hrynyk 1948 Report).

8. Ukrainian Insurgent Army (UPA)—a military arm of the Ukrainian Supreme Liberation Council (UHVR) formed by the OUN (the Bandera faction) and its allies in 1944. Dating since 1941, UPA was "taken over" by the Bandera OUN in 1942. See John Armstrong, *Ukrainian Nationalism*, 2nd ed. (Littleton, Colo., 1980), 6.

9. Organization of Ukrainian Nationalists (OUN), established in 1929, was a western-Ukraine-based underground nationalist movement, which split in 1940 when the younger and more radical faction in the OUN leadership, led by Stefan Bandera, repudiated the leadership of Colonel Andrii Melnyk, who succeeded the OUN's founding leader, Colonel Ievhen Konovalets after his assassination by an NKVD agent in 1938. The Bandera faction soon captured the allegiance of the majority of OUN members in Galicia. See Armstrong, op. cit., 35–64.

10. On Soviet attempts to force the Lithuanian Roman Catholic bishops and clergy to break away from the Vatican, see V. Stanley Vardys, *The Catholic Church, Dissent and Nationality in Soviet Lithuania* (Boulder, Colo., 1978), ch. 5.

11. The demand was made by a Soviet high command spokesman to Metropolitan Slipyi's delegation when it visited Moscow in December 1944 (interview with Cardinal Slipyi, Rome, February 26, 1975). The church could not directly intervene in the fierce struggle between the UPA and Soviet security forces. Metropolitan Slipyi nevertheless appealed to the faithful to observe the fifth commandment and the obligation of Christian charity. Subsequently, the Lviv see arranged for a secret meeting in late February 1945 between representatives of the Soviet forces and the UPA command, which failed to end hostilities in the western Ukraine, as the former demanded an unconditional surrender of the Ukrainian insurgents, an "offer" that was bound to be

turned down by UPA/OUN (Metropolitan Iosyf Slipyi, "Zhaloba," a complaint to a minister of the Ukrainian SSR, dated February 17, 1961, written while the metropolitan was in Kiev prison undergoing another interrogation; a copy of this document was received from Cardinal Slipyi in November 1981). Cf. Lev Shankovskyi, "Bolshevyky pro UPA," *Visnyk O.Ch.S.U.*, vol. XXII, no. 6 (1968), 18, and his "Fantazii Moskvy pro roliu Vatykanu u borotbi UPA," *Patriiarkhat*, vol. XI, no. 3 (March 1978), 15–16; and Serhii T. Danylenko, *Dorohoiu hanby i zrady* (Kiev, 1972), 260–262.

12. This is suggested by the absence of any appeal for "reunion" with Russian Orthodoxy in the first published attack on the Greek Catholic church on April 6, 1945 (Volodymyr Rosovych [pseudonym of Iaroslav Halan], "Z khrestom chy nozhem?," in the Lviv daily *Vilna Ukraina*), and by a highly publicized meeting in the Kremlin, on April 10, 1945, between Stalin and Molotov, on the one side, and Patriarch Aleksii, who was accompanied by Metropolitan Nikolai of Krutitsy and Protopresbyter N. F. Kolchitskii, executive director of the patriarchate, on the other. Moscow patriarchate, *Patriarkh Sergii i ego dukhovnoe nasledstvo* (Moscow, 1947), 376.

13. Leonid Il'ich Brezhenev, hitherto the political commissar of the 18th Army, was sent to the western Ukraine as chief of political administration of the Subcarpathian Military District some time in late May or June 1945, and remained in this post until after the liquidation of the Uniate church.

14. Budka was born June 7, 1877 in Dobromirka, Galicia, ordained on October 14, 1905, and consecrated titular bishop of Patara on July 15, 1912. He served as apostolic exarch for Greek Catholics in Canada from 1912 to 1927. Upon his return to Lviv, he became an auxiliary bishop and vicar-general of the Lviv archdiocese. Sentenced in summer 1946 to eight years of forced labor, Bishop Budka died in Karaganda on October 1, 1949. See A. Pekar, *Ispovidnyky viry nashoi suchasnosty* (Toronto-Rome, 1982), 78–82.

15. Charnetskyi was born on December 14, 1884, in Semakivtsi, Galicia; he was ordained in 1909, taught at the Stanyslaviv theological seminary from 1910 to 1919, joined the Redemptorist order in 1919, and was appointed abbot of the Kostopol monastery in Volyn in 1926. He was named in 1931 as apostolic visitor for the Uniates in Volyn, Polissia, Kholm, and Pidliashshia regions, and ordained as titular bishop of Lebedo with residence in Kovel. Forced to leave Volyn in 1939, he resided in Lviv until his arrest in 1945. Sentenced in 1946 to ten years, Bishop Charnetsky returned to Lviv in 1956 and died there on April 2, 1959. See (Bakhtalovskyi) Stefan-Iosyf, *Nykolai Charnetskyi, ChNI: Iepyskop-spovidnyk* (Yorkton, Sask., 1980).

16. Khomyshyn was born on March 25, 1867 in Hadynkivtsi, Galicia. Ordained in 1893, he earned a doctorate in theology from Vienna University in 1899, and was appointed rector of the Lviv theological seminary in 1902. Ordained Bishop of Stanyslaviv in 1904, Khomyshyn

became known as the chief spokesman for the "Western" orientation in
the Greek Catholic church. Sentenced in 1946 to ten years, he died in the
Kiev prison on January 17, 1947. See Petro Melnychuk, *Vladyka Hryhorii
Khomyshyn: Patriot-Misionar-Muchenyk* (Rome-Philadelphia, 1979).

17. Liatyshevskyi was born on October 17, 1879 in Bohorodchany,
Galicia. He studied theology in Lviv, Innsbruck, and Vienna, earning a
doctorate in theology. Ordained in 1907, Liatyshevskyi was consecrated
as titular bishop of Adada and auxiliary to Bishop Khomyshyn of
Stanyslaviv in January 1930. Sentenced in 1946 to eight years, he
returned in June 1955 to Stanislav (Ivano-Frankivsk) and died there in
November 1957. See Pekar, op. cit., 86–89.

18. See "Pro likvidatsiiu ukrainskoi katolytskoi Tserkvy" (apparently
written on the basis of information provided by the late Cardinal Slipyi),
in *Martyrolohiia Ukrainskykh Tserkov*; vol. II: *Ukrainska Katolytska
Tserkva*, comp. and ed. by Osyp Zinkevych and Reverend Taras R.
Lonchyna (Toronto-Baltimore, 1985), 240. This source refers to April 1945
as the date of mass arrests that were to clear the way for the "Action
Group" headed by Reverend H. Kostelnyk. The figure of 100 arrested
priests was supplied by Kostelnyk himself in his letter to OUN
underground, written in the fall of 1946, under the pseudonym "Father
Author" (Kostelnyk's use of this pseudonym in his communication with
OUN was confirmed by Mykola Lebid). The letter was transmitted to
OUN leaders in the Drohobych *oblast* by "Father Ikona" (possibly the
local Orthodox bishop, Mykhail Melnyk). A copy of an OUN report on a
secret meeting with the latter, including a transcript of Kostelnyk's letter,
was preserved in the ZP UHVR archives in New York ("Do t. zv.
'voz'iednannia' tserkov," file F3-1). Among those arrested was the
Reverend Petro Verhun. Born on November 18, 1890, he was ordained in
1927, and served as pastor and, from 1940 as apostolic visitor for
Ukrainian Greek Catholics in Germany. Arrested in Berlin after its
capture by the Soviet troops, Reverend Verhun was brought to the Kiev
NKGB prison and tried together with the Lviv episcopate in summer
1946. Sentenced to eight years of forced labor, he was released only in
1955, but was committed to exile in Krasnoiarsk krai in Siberia, where he
died on February 7, 1957.

19. Havryil Kostelnyk (1886–1948), native of the Backa (a
Ruthenian/Ukrainian-populated region in what is now northeastern
Yugoslavia), emerged in the late 1920s as a principal critic of the
Vatican's Uniate policy and the leading representative of the "Eastern"
(antilatinization) orientation among the Greek Catholic clergy in Galicia.
His position made him an object of the NKVD pressure and blackmail
already during the 1939–1941 occupation, with the Soviet authorities
eager but unable to have Kostelnyk organize an "away from Rome"
schism in the Ukrainian Greek Catholic church. After the Soviet
reoccupation of Galicia and the arrest of the entire Ukrainian Catholic
episcopate, Kostelnyk—a long-standing opponent of Iosyf Slipyi—was

finally compelled by the authorities to assume chairmanship of the "Action Group."

20. Even before it was "officially recognized" by the Soviet government, the "Action Group" stated in its public appeal to the Uniate clergy, on May 28, 1945, that it was formed "by permission of the state authorities" and that the latter "will recognize only the directives of our Action Group, and will not recognize any other administrative authority within the Greek Catholic church." *Diiannia Soboru hreko-katolytskoi tserkvy u Lvovi 8–10 bereznia 1946* (Lviv: Vydannia Prezydii Soboru, 1946), 23. On behalf of the Council of People's Commissars of the Ukrainian SSR, the republican commissioner of the Council for Affairs of the Russian Orthodox church, P. Khodchenko, replied on June 18 that the "Action Group for Reunion of the Greek Catholic church is being SANCTIONED with your present membership as the ONLY provisional organ of church administration, which is authorized to direct all affairs of the existing Greek Catholic parishes in the western *oblasti* of the Ukraine and to carry on the task of reunion of the above parishes with the Russian Orthodox church," and ordered the "Group" to provide him with the "lists of all deans, parish priests and superiors of monasteries who refuse to submit to the jurisdiction of the Action Group" (ibid., 19–20; emphasis supplied). The government's intervention violated both the Soviet constitution and its own legislation on religious "cults." After the bishops' arrest, before the surfacing of the "Action Group," Kostelnyk was appointed by the Soviet authorities as "administrator of the church" (ibid., 35). It appears that Kostelnyk was also arrested for one week, and produced a personal "declaration" that was subsequently cited by Soviet anti-Uniate writers with access to NKGB/procuracy files (e.g., Danylenko, *Dorohoiu hanby i zrady*, 298). It is very likely that, while imprisoned, Kostelnyk was finally "persuaded" by the NKGB to assume leadership of the "Action Group." On Kostelnyk's arrest, see Iu. Gerych, "Iak vidbuvsia vozsoedinitelnyi sobor u Lvovi, 8 bereznia 1946 (Na osnovi svidchen uchasnyka)," *Kalendar 'Svitla'...1955* (Toronto, 1955), 88. It is clear from the fragment of Kostelnyk's "declaration" cited by Danylenko and Dmytruk, that the former then believed that his two sons, who had volunteered for the Waffen SS Division "Galicia" in 1943, were either dead or held captive by the Soviet forces. Only some time later, Kostelnyk learned that his sons survived the war and were in the West.

21. The arrests and the imposition of the conversionist "Action Group" in place of the Church's legitimate leadership evoked, on July 1, a letter of protest to the Soviet government, reportedly signed by 300 priests. They pleaded for the release of the metropolitan and other bishops and for the right (denied to them by the authorities) to select in the meantime an authentic Greek Catholic administration for the metropoly, as provided by the canon law. The priests' appeal was ignored by the government which now brought the entire "reunion" campaign into the open by publishing, on July 6, in the Lviv daily *Vilna Ukraina*,

both the "Action Group's" May 28 letter to the Soviet Ukrainian government and the latter's "response" of June 18. The July 1 protest is cited in full in Ivan Hryniokh, "Znyshchennia Ukrainskoi Katolytskoi Tserkvy rosiisko-bolshevytskym rezhymom," *Suchasnist*, vol. X, no. 9 (September 1970), 53–54.

22. For first-hand accounts of the NKGB's "conversion" action, see the Hrynyk 1948 Report, 1–28.

23. According to a report by the Reverend A. Pelvetskyi on the opening day of the *sobor*, 986 priests in the four Galician *oblasti* had "joined the Action Group" by 8 March 1945; he claimed that 281 priests refused to "join" the "Group" (implying that they were still at large); the number of "recalcitrants" listed by Pelvetskyi obviously omitted those who were already imprisoned by the Soviet police (ibid., 61).

24. In the course of seemingly unending "transmission-belt-style" interrogations by a team of investigators in the NKGB prison in Kiev, Slipyi was repeatedly offered the post of the Orthodox metropolitan of Kiev, in exchange for his "voluntary" renunciation of the union with Rome (interview with Cardinal Slipyi, Rome, February 26, 1975).

25. *Diiannia*, 28–31. The problem (which Soviet and the Moscow patriarchate's accounts have not been able to resolve ever since, without falsifying either facts or canons) is, however, that the presence of *Orthodox* bishops (even if they were former Uniate priests) at a Greek Catholic *sobor*, convened without the authority and in the absence of Greek Catholic bishops, could not make such a gathering legitimate from the viewpoint of *either* Catholic or Orthodox canons (just as the presence of Catholic bishops at an Orthodox *sobor* convened under analogous circumstances would not make the latter canonical).

26. *Vilna Ukraina* (Lviv), March 1, 1946.

27. According to *Diiannia*, 32, 225 "invitations" were produced and "sent out" to "priest-delegates" and twenty-two "lay guests" only after the "reunited" thirteen members of the Action Group returned from Kiev on February 26, leaving thus only six to seven days for the entire "organizational work," as the pre-*sobor* meeting of twenty core "delegates" took place on March 6 (when "the entire *sobor* agenda was accepted"), while "delegates" were supposed to arrive on March 7 (ibid., 32–33). The sudden haste must have been caused by the decision in the Kremlin to proceed with the liquidation of the union with Rome, conveyed to the Kiev and Galicia authorities probably no sooner than after February 10. It is perhaps no coincidence that this sudden acceleration of the Soviet timetable followed the regime's "electoral victory" on February 10 in the first postwar "elections" to the Supreme Soviet, which were to demonstrate the "monolithic support" for government in the "reunited" western Ukraine. In Galicia, elections were preceded by a near total blockade—the stationing of troops in towns and all but a few villages to prevent the popular boycott of the vote, called for by UPA/OUN. Subsequently, the Soviet authorities issued another (the

fifth) appeal to the UPA/OUN members to surrender in return for amnesty; cf. Yaroslav Bilinsky, *The Second Soviet Republic: The Ukraine After World War II* (New Brunswick, N.J., 1964), 131–132. It may be assumed that the Action Group's stay in Kiev (February 20-25) involved planning for the Lviv *sobor* with the security officials and the Moscow patriarchate representatives, with hardly anything left to chance.

28. *Diiannia*, 32–52. It is not accidental that the Moscow patriarchate's multilingual "document collection" *Lvivskyi Tserkovnyi Sobor: Dokumenty i materialy, 1946–1981* (Kiev, 1984), eliminated from the original *Diiannia* most of the embarrassing documents and passages, including the Action Group's appeal to the Soviet government and, the most compromising, Khodchenko's letter of June 18, 1945, confirming on behalf of the government the exclusive authority of this NKGB-handpicked group to usurp the powers of the arrested bishops and to bring about the Greek Catholic church's incorporation into the Russian Orthodox church. For more detail, see Ivan Hvat's review of *Lvivskyi Tserkovnyi Sobor* (1984) in *Suchasnist*, vol. 25, no. 1 (January 1985), 111–118.

29. "Do t. zv. 'voz'iednannia' tserkov," 1, 4, 5. Cf. Klym. Ie. Dmytruk, *Pid shtandartamy reaktsii i fashyzmu* (Kiev, 1976), 287–288.

30. Interviews with Kostelnyk family members. Kostelnyk's assassin was shot from the car that was waiting for him to make his escape. The police insisted that Kostelnyk's widow identify the corpse (dressed up in an SS uniform!) as one of their missing sons (who had joined the SS Division "Galicia" and was held in a British POW camp), but she denied that it was he. Subsequently, the corpse had reportedly disappeared from the morgue. Danylenko, after reconstructing a fictional conversation between "Vatican intelligence agents" and Ukrainian nationalist leaders—during which the "candidacy" of Kostelnyk's son was considered and dismissed—alleged that the assassin was an "OUNite," Vasyl Pankiv (pseudonym "Iaremko"). Danylenko, op. cit., 309–312. No Ukrainian nationalist groups ever claimed credit for this act.

31. This is essentially the argument pursued by "Father Author" (Kostelnyk) in his letter to the UPA-OUN leaders, cited in "Do t. zv. 'voz'iednannia' tserkov."

32. For an assessment of the losses suffered by the Orthodox church in the Ukraine under Khrushchev, see my article "The Orthodox Church and the Soviet Regime in the Ukraine, 1953–1971," *Canadian Slavonic Papers*, vol. 45, no. 2 (Summer 1972), 101–212.

33. See Pekar, op. cit., 73, 88–89.

34. See Ie. Shtendera and P. Potichnyi, eds., *Litopys UPA*, vol. 13, I: *Peremyshchyna: Peremyskyi kurin UPA* (Toronto, 1986), xxiv–xxvii.

35. V. Kubiiovych, "Ukraintsi v korinnii Polshchi," in *Entsyklopediia ukrainoznavstva*, vol. 6 (Munich, 1970), 2253.

36. *Hrynyk 1948 Report*, 15–17, 87–91. Hrynyk was arrested by the UB (Polish internal security police) along with Bishop Kotsylovskyi in

September 1945. On January 16, 1946, they were handed over to the NKGB, but on January 24 they were inexplicably released and transported back to Peremyshl after rather cursory interrogations in the border town of Mostyska. It seems that this attempted deportation of Bishop Kotsylovskyi was undertaken on Polish rather than Soviet initiative, unlike the second arrest and deportation of Bishops Kotsylovskyi and Lakota in late June 1946. (Hrynyk barely managed to escape arrest that time.)

37. The plenary session lasted from May 22 to 24. See the group photograph of participating bishops, including Kotsylovskyi and Lakota in Peter Reina, *Stefan Kardynal Wyszynski, Prymas Polski*, vol. I (London, 1979), between 320 and 321. According to his biographer, Bishop Kotsylovskyi, anticipating his fate, had written during the Częstochowa session a declaration (left apparently with his Roman Catholic hosts, for transmission to the pope): "At the feet of Christ's vicar, Pope Pius XII, I submit the declaration of my loyalty, respect, and filial love and ask him to delegate me to die for the Holy Union." Cited in Reverend Irenei Nazarko, *Iosafat Kotsylovskyi, Ch.S.V.V., Iepyskop peremyskyi* (Toronto, 1954), 46.

38. For a description of the June 1946 arrests, see *Hrynyk 1948 Report*, 15–17.

39. Ibid., 58–59, 151–153.

40. Ibid., 44–45.

41. Ibid., 80. Pekar, op. cit., 64–65.

42. *Hrynyk 1948 Report*, 43–44. Initially, Hrynyk was appointed as vicar-general for the Peremyshl diocese, while Reverend Andrii Zlupko was made vicar-general for the apostolic administration of Lemkivshchyna. After the forcible removal of Ukrainians from southern Poland and their dispersal in the former German territories in northern Poland, Hrynyk could not effectively carry out his responsibilities until after "Polish October" in 1956. Father Hrynyk died in 1977.

43. See Myroslav Trukhan, "Aktsiia Visla," *Vidnova*, no. 3 (Summer-Fall 1985): 53–62.

44. Ibid., 161.

45. I. Blum, "Udzial Wojska Polskiego w walce o utrwalenie władzy ludowej," Wojskowy Przeglad Historyczny (Warsaw, 1959), cited in Trukhan, loc. cit., 59. Blum reports that as a result of Operation Vistula April 17–July 31, 1947), "2,781 active Ukrainian fascists" were sent to the "isolation camp." The data on the Ukrainian Catholic clergy in Jaworzno are listed in *Hrynyk 1948 Report*, 115–121. According to a memorandum submitted by branches of the Ukrainian Social Cultural Society (the only Ukrainian organization recognized in Poland since 1956) to the Sixth Congress of the PZPR, imprisonment in Jaworzno camp was indiscriminate and "every attempt to return from the western provinces to native areas in 1947–1949 ended with commitment to the camp in Jaworzno." "Memorial ukrainski do VI Zjazdu PZPR," *Kultura*, no. 5/308

(1973): 69, 77. Local Ukrainians estimated as many as 5,000 Ukrainian "internees" at Jaworzno.

46. *Hrynyk 1948 Report*, 122–127.

47. Ibid., 84–114. Cf. O.P.Kh., "Dolia Ukrainskoi Hreko-katolytskoi tserkvy v Polshchi" (cited hereafter as "Dolia ukrainskoi"), *Nasha meta* (Toronto), May 11, 1957.

48. Makarii's transfer to Poland's "Autocephalous [independent] Orthodox church" posed a canonical problem, which was "resolved" in a rather unusual way: in April 1951, the synod of bishops of the church in Poland resolved that it had "no worthy candidate" in its midst for the post of metropolitan of Warsaw and all Poland; accordingly, the synod asked the Moscow patriarchate for a "worthy candidate," with Moscow "releasing" Archbishop Makarii Oksiiuk of Lviv and Ternopil, who was installed as the head of the Polish Orthodox church on July 8, 1951. A. A. Bogolepov, *Tserkov' pod vlastiu kommunizma* (Institut po izucheniiu SSSR, issledovaniia i materialy, series I, vol. 42) (Munich, 1958), 165–166.

49. *Dziennik ustaw*, 1947, no. 59: 318.

50. Ibid., 1949, no. 53: 404.

51. Michal Pietrzak, *Prawo wyznaniowe* (Warsaw, 1978), 113–114.

52. The Union of Uzhhorod (1646) was renounced and the Mukachiv diocese in the Carpathian Ukraine annexed to the Russian Orthodox church on August 28, 1949, by an "act of reunion" read out during a service by a "converted" pastor of the Uniate diocesan cathedral, Reverend Irenei Kondratovych. No equivalent of the Lviv *sobor* was attempted in this diocese, where the MGB "missionary" activities on behalf of the Moscow patriarchate have encountered much more determined resistance by the clergy and believers. See Vasyl Markus, *Nyshchennia Hreko-Katolytskoi Tserkvy v Mukachivskii leparkhii v 1945–1950 rr.* (Offprint from a volume dedicated to the memory of Z. Kuzelia, *Zapysky N.T.Sh.*, vol. CLXIX (Paris, 1962); and Pekar, op. cit., 175–234. Prior to its suppression, the Mukachiv diocese embraced, in 1944, a bishop, 281 parishes with 459 churches, 354 secular and 13 monastic priests, 5 monasteries with 35 monks, 3 convents with 50 nuns, a theological seminary with 85 students, and 461,555 believers. *Annuario Pontificio per l'anno 1965* (Vatican City, 1965), 288.

53. Cf. Dominik Morawski, "Korespondencja z Rzymu," *Kultura*, no. 5/308 (1973): 51.

54. *Hrynyk 1948 Report*, 84–114. Cf. O.P.Kh., "Dolia ukrainskoi."

55. *Hrynyk 1948 Report*, 29–30, 154. Hrynyk, as well as more recent sources from Poland, noted that the Polish Ministry of Internal Affairs (which "oversees" religious groups and national minorities) had been facilitating Orthodox conversion activities among the much more discrimated against Greek Catholics to the extent of allowing Orthodox clergy to capitalize on the frustration and bitterness of Ukrainian Catholics over the intolerance and chauvinism of the local Polish Catholic clergy.

56. For a detailed account of the negotiations by the two senior canons of the Peremyshl diocese (Fathers M. Ripetski and V. Hrynyk) with the governmental Department of Confessions and Primate Wyszynski during November 1956, see O.P.Kh., "Dolia ukrainskoi."

57. G. Barberini, M. Stoehr, and E. Weingaertner, eds., *Kirche im Sozialismus* (Frankfurt a. M., 1977), 277. By 1977, Greek Catholics were identified as such in 156 parishes of the Roman Catholic church, the largest concentrations being in the following dioceses: Warmia (40), Wrocław (35), Koszalin-Kołobrzeg (29), Gorzów (12), Tarnów (9), Przemyśl (7). Since 1945, out of some 350 former Greek Catholic churches, 92 were appropriated by the Roman Catholic church. *Kościół Katolicki w Polsce, 1945–1972* comp. by Witold Zdaniewicz (Poznań-Warszawa, 1978 ["For internal use only"]), tables 4 (86), 59, 78.

58. Tymothiusz Klempski, "Matka świetych Polska," *Kultura*, no. 3 (1981): 25. Cf. Vasyl Kachmar, "Ukraintsi v Polshchi," *Svoboda* (Jersey City, N.J.), September 16, 17, 18, 1975; and Czesław Kijanka, "Prychynok do dyskusii pro polsko-ukrainski stosunky," *Suchasnist*, vol. XXV, no. 4 (April 1985): 113–119.

59. *Czarna księga cenzury PRL* (London, 1977), 75.

60. See my article "The Catacomb Church: Ukrainian Greek Catholics in the USSR," *Religion in Communist Lands*, vol. 5, no. 1 (Spring 1977): 4–12.

61. The Polish minister for religious affairs, A. Lopatka, admitted at a public discussion in Gdańsk, in May 1985, that the Greek Catholic *church* "does not exist" in Poland, but only a "Greek Catholic *rite*" *within* the Polish Roman Catholic church, which, he claimed, "does not obstruct its activities, as shown by recent visit by Archbishop Marusyn." In contradiction to known facts, Lopatka alleged that "nobody applied to the government for a legal status for the Greek Catholic church." *Nashe slovo* (Warsaw), May 26, 1985.

62. See, in particular, Ivan Hvat, "The Ukrainian Catholic Church, the Vatican, and the Soviet Union During the Pontificate of John Paul II," *Religion in Communist Lands*, vol. XI, no. 3 (Winter 1983): 264–280; Tadeusz Zychiewicz, "Konstantynopol, Moskiew, Unia, Papierz," *Kultura*, no. 9/396 (1980): esp. 22–25; and Dominik Morawski, "Kościół ukrainski widziany z Rzymu," ibid., no. 9/1982: esp. 86–89.

63. Two priests were ordained by Archbishop Myroslav-Ivan Liubachivskyi (then coadjutor of the archbishop-major of Lviv, Cardinal Josyf Slipyi) in 1981; five during Archbishop Myroslav Marusyn's official visit to Poland as secretary of the Congregation for Eastern Churches (June 21–July 7, 1984), and another five during his second official visit, (June 27–July 28, 1985). All ordinations were held in Peremyshl. See *Pamiatka arkhyiereiskykh vidvidyn* (Rome, 1985); and O. Matsiivskyi, "Druha pastyrska podorozh arkhyiepyskopa Myroslava do Polshchi," *Novyi shliakh* (Toronto), August 17, 1985.

64. In the fall of 1985, there were fifty Greek Catholic priests,

including thirteen Basilians, serving seventy-six "pastoral points" in Poland. See an interview with Father Iosafat Romanyk, provincial of the Basilian order in Poland and vicar-general for Greek Catholics in northern Poland, in *Wież*, November 1985, reproduced in *Informations-Dienst des katholischen Arbeitskreises für zeitgeschichtliche Fragen* (Bonn), no. 136 (1985): 17.

65. In 1985, there were fifteen Ukrainian Catholic seminarians studying in Lublin and nine Basilian seminarians in Warsaw. Ibid., 72. Rejuvenation of the Ukrainian Greek Catholic clergy in Poland was long overdue; in 1979, out of forty-three priests twenty-three were over seventy, four over sixty, three over fifty, seven over forty, and only six below forty years of age.

66. Kazimierz Polanski, "Bilorusy—lytovtsi—ukraintsi: Nashi vorohy chy braty?", *Vidnova*, no. 3 (Summer-Fall 1985): 269n. At the same time (1984), forty-five Ukrainian Catholic priests were active in Poland. Except for the Basilian church in Warsaw, none of the churches utilized by Ukrainian Catholics are owned by the Greek Catholic church, as it has no legal status and no property rights.

67. Amidst an intensified persecution of Ukrainian Catholics in the Soviet Union, an "Action Group for the Defense of Believers and the Church in the Ukraine" was formed in September 1982 by Iosyf Terelia and Father Hryhorii Budzinskyi, Vasyl Kobryn, and several others. The group has publicized new documentation about the mistreatment of the illegal Ukrainian Greek Catholic church by the Soviet authorities who continue to refuse "registration" of the Uniate congregations under a strange argument that this church "does not exist," since it has "dissolved itself" at the Lviv *sobor* in 1946. At the very same time, the clergy of this "nonexistent" church are being fined and arrested for ministering to the "nonexistent" Uniate believers ("violation of the law on cults"). In 1985, Vasyl Kobryn was sentenced to three years, and Iosyf Terelia to seven years of forced labor and five years exile. See *Martyrolohiia*, 651–672, 683–730; *For My Name's Sake: Selections from the Writings of Iosyf Terelia*, ed. Andrew Sorokowski (Keston, 1986); and Michael Dymyd, "The Ukrainian Catholic Church in the USSR," *Smoloskyp* (Ellicott City, Md.), vol. 7, no. 29 (Spring 1986): 20–22. For samples of defamation campaign against members of the "Action Group" carried on in the local Soviet press, see S. Brukhal, "Pid maskoiu relihii," *Vilna Ukraina* (Lviv), January 7, 1986; and A. Lysiuk, "Shum porozhnei bochki: Komu i dlia chego on ponadobilsia," *Lvovskaia pravda* (Lviv), April 3, 1985.

# Index

# Contributors

**Book Editor**
Dennis J. Dunn *Southwest Texas State University*

**General Editor**
**Publications of the Third World Congress**
**for Soviet and East European Studies**
R. C. Elwood *Carleton University*

John D. Basil *University of South Carolina*

Bohdan R. Bociurkiw *Carleton University*

Fred Hahn *Columbia University*

Jure Krišto *Aquinas College*

Edward D. Wynot, Jr. *Florida State University*